Design,
Create,
AND Quilt

Design, Create, and Quilt

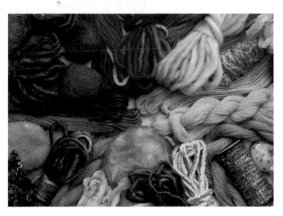

How to
Design a Quilt—
Lessons,
Techniques,
and Patterns

ROSE HUGHES

Martingale®
Create with Confidence

Design, Create, and Quilt: How to Design a Quilt—
Lessons, Techniques, and Patterns
© 2012 by Rose Hughes

Martingale®
19021 120th Ave. NE, Ste. 102
Bothell, WA 98011-9511 USA
ShopMartingale.com

MISSION STATEMENT

Dedicated to providing quality products and service to inspire creativity.

Printed in China

17 16 15 14 13 12   8 7 6 5 4 3 2 1

Library of Congress Cataloging-in-Publication Data is available upon request.

ISBN: 978-1-60468-174-1

CREDITS:

President & CEO: Tom Wierzbicki
Editor in Chief: Mary V. Green
Design Director: Paula Schlosser
Managing Editor: Karen Costello Soltys
Technical Editor: Nancy Mahoney
Copy Editor: Melissa Bryan
Production Manager: Regina Girard
Illustrator: Christine Erikson
Cover Designer: Paula Schlosser
Text Designer: Connor Chin
Photographer: Brent Kane

Acknowledgments

I want to give really big thanks to everyone who has made my journey of writing and sharing such a rewarding experience. Many, many people contributed to this journey—new friendships were made, and older relationships were expanded and enriched along the way.

A big thank-you to members of my family who are always there and always supportive, and to all the people at Martingale who are fun to work with, and fun to laugh with too! This book contains information that can only come through interaction. My design group—Joanell Connolly, Jeanette Kelly, Karen Gray, and Susan Willen—took a grand, interactive, creative leap with me. There was also a group of friends that participated in the big Sew-In and stitched many of the quilt tops found here. Jake Finch, Sam Hunter, and Vicki Tymcyszyn were there to share the stitching, fun, and food. Natalie Barnes was there too, and I am especially grateful to her for all the time she spent stitching alongside me after the big community sewing day.

There were others as well, students and teachers with whom I was delighted to share creative time throughout my many travels. The journey is amazing and continues to bring joy to my heart with each turn in the road. Thank you!

Contents

Replenishing
Your Creativity

In my 20th year of quilting, I started to reflect on what it means to me to be a quilter. Looking back over this long period of time, one expects to have seen some changes, and I'm tickled (maybe not pink) to be able to say that I have been a witness to and a part of (OK, an instigator of) many quilterly changes.

I feel lucky that I started quilting at a time when many stitchers were jumping in with their love of fabric to create works for personal, nonutilitarian expression. There was no secret handshake, just quilters young and old, female and male, seasoned and brand new, as well as tons of non-quilters who chose to "do their own thing." Some of these works were just short steps away from the traditional utilitarian creations that had been in favor for generations, while others stretched, bent, and sometimes turned our common materials of fabric, thread, needles, and batting right on their heads. There was a debate about just what to call yourself if you were part of this group—"art quilter," or "fiber artist"? Even at this point there are many variations.

While we were debating about what to call ourselves, more than 30 years passed by. That was time enough for a new group of quilters to spring forth with a fresh vision and a whole new debate on what to call their type of quilting. We most often hear them referred to as "modern quilters." It's refreshing and exciting to see their works and listen to them debate.

Is there really anything new happening? Personally, I say yes, and I believe that the quilters of a hundred years ago or more might chuckle at being called "traditional." Quilters who came before us, were just like us. We all take the materials and tools that are available in our own time and relish the magic of turning pieces of fabric into art. We turn fabric into things of beauty that may keep us warm or decorate our homes. We turn fabric into quilts. Quilters, no matter what we call ourselves, all have certain things in common, but at the very top of the list is our love of fabric and the use of needles, thread, and batting to create.

My own quilting journey began once I saw my first quilt, touched the fabrics, and ran my hand along the lines of stitching. Love at first sight. I had no choice but to pick up a needle and try my hand at creating this magic for myself. I was lucky to catch the quilting bug when I did. For one thing, rotary cutters were already being used. Also, I lived close enough to San Francisco that I had access to an amazing source of inspiration: a collection of Amish quilts that was on display in the offices of the clothing manufacturer Esprit during the 1990s. I visited this collection many times, amazed to see firsthand how the Amish quilters used their fabrics and how the simplicity and graphic quality of their designs mixed with the perfection of their tiny quilting

"By the Light of the Moon"—this quilt is one that is close to my heart and always hangs above the fireplace in my studio. It was made to commemorate our 10-year wedding anniversary celebration with my husband, David, in Mendocino, California. There amongst the redwoods the ravens played, and we took moonlit strolls under star-filled skies. It's also one of the very first times I used the construction method I now call Fast-Pieced Appliqué to create simple curves, and check out all the beads.

stitches. This and so much more fed my desire to work with solid-colored fabrics and to learn to push the needle in and out to create my own tiny quilting stitches. I was hooked, and the love of the Amish geometric patterns and use of solid fabrics kept me happily stitching for some time.

Then, as many of you already know, I really wanted to add some twisting, swerving, bending curves. It ushered in a move away from stitching quilts for utilitarian reasons, but I would never leave my fabric, needles, thread, and batting behind! This desire took my quilting journey into whole new areas. Now, 20 years later, with all the twists and turns my own work has taken, I believe I've never really traveled far from that love of the graphic quality the designs presented and the use of the quilting stitch for its quality of simple definition, texture, and utility.

Maybe you're out there reading this and saying to yourself, "Come on, Rose, what about all that embellishment stuff?" To you I would respond, just take another look. Admittedly, shine does bring out the devil in me, but even my use of beads and embellishments closely follows a quilter's purpose of definition, texture, and utility.

In the middle of a huge project in my corporate life, I was introduced to the writings of Dr. Clarissa Pinkola Estés, including her book *Women Who Run with the Wolves* (Ballantine Books, 1996). Have you heard of it? I found understanding and inspiration in her words and her capable storytelling. In another of her works, *The Creative Fire: Myths and Stories on the Cycles of*

Creativity (Sounds True, 1993), she shares her concept of the cyclical nature of creativity and provides examples from mythology. The underlying lesson of these tales is that things run in cycles. *Life* runs in cycles, and as I sought out curves and other unique methods to stitch my ideas together, I was introduced to the idea of creative cycles.

Creative cycles—the ups and downs of knowing just how to do something is mixed in with the feeling that you have no clue at all about how to make a wonderful quilt. It was through the storytelling of Dr. Pinkola Estés that the need to learn a bit, think on it a bit, and then create a bit started to make sense.

One of the things I took away from mythological tales about creativity is that everything is somehow connected—connected and recycled. Old becomes new once again.

IDEAS

As I went through the mythological stories of Dr. Pinkola Estés and let their message sink in, I tried to come up with a way to remember this lesson. This is when the IDEAS acronym came to me.

I= Incubation

D= Design

E= Execution

A= Assessment

S= Start all over

As you glance at this book's table of contents, you'll find that the book has a section for each of the basic design elements: line, shape, texture, color, space, and composition. In each section, one of these elements has guided the projects, big or small, but since I believe that the doors, windows, and keyholes of your mind should always be open to discovery, you'll find the design element defined, along with a few short designing exercises. Try out the exercises before diving into the projects.

Besides being inspired by the individual design elements, the projects are built around the idea of mixing Fast-Piece Appliqué with traditional and modern methods of quilt construction and ideas.

I'm constantly looking for new quilting ideas, forever replenishing and resetting my own creative cycle back to the beginning, to start all over again. I hope this book will help guide you toward that same feeling, by describing many, many opportunities to replenish and keep your own creative cycle rolling along. You never know when that little bit of new information flowing in may percolate and burst forth, presenting itself as a huge new creative opportunity.

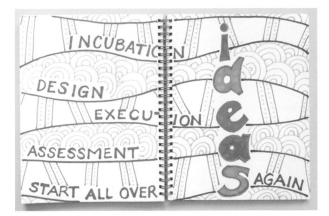

Pages from my old sketchbook where I played with these ideas of creative cycles

Let's Artify!

I have always loved art, quilts, and words. And in this book, I wanted to mix all of these loves together. For me, words have a way of either getting directly to the heart of something, or making my imagination swirl with possibilities. So, it seems natural that when I began to think about mixing things up, and sharing my feelings regarding art and quilts, I started by mixing words.

Including *art* as my first word was a given. I'd like to say that the right word to mix with it came quickly, but it didn't. I wanted a word that would instill a challenge to build your art muscles and to open yourself up to creative possibilities. It took some time, but the right word, the perfect partner to art, finally came to me and that word was *fortify*.

Art, a noun, is the word we use to describe works that, through our skill and imagination, we create to share with others. Fortify, a verb, is a word that calls us to action, and when I checked the dictionary for the definition, the words *encourage, reassure, brace, embolden,* and *reinforce* came up. Perfect words to keep in mind as we artify: boldly build our art muscles.

I meet many people while I'm teaching. Some are reluctant to trust themselves when it comes to picking colors or designing, while others are ready and willing to jump in and try new methods. It's important to realize that to artify ourselves takes practice. Luckily, a little goes a long way, so throughout this book everyone will get small bits of practice opportunity.

In each section I have gone back to the design basics: line, shape, texture, color, space, and composition. For each of these subjects I have provided a few artify exercises. Each has been fully tested by my own small design group, and each provides a bit of a warm-up. These short lessons are designed to help build, or reinforce, our understanding of basic design elements and increase our sense of what does and doesn't work—letting us learn to listen to our inner voice.

Try them out, and then you can take those artified lesson ideas and quiltify them. After all, we are quilters, and quilters have the common desire to enjoy, love, and share fabric!

ARTIFY

ar•ti•fy (verb)

1. strengthen by learning basic art elements and design principles

2. open ourselves to new ways of seeing the world around us

3. encourage others and share ideas with fresh new vision

Tools for Artification

All of the artify lessons in this book have been kept deliberately simple, allowing you to use materials you already have or can easily find. I'd like you to be open to new tools (these may be old tools, but new to you) and new processes, for with each will come new experiences and possibilities.

- White multipurpose paper
- Colored paper or old magazines
- Scissors
- Glue stick
- Pencils
- Markers
- Watercolor set or InkTense pencils
- Paintbrushes
- Mixing palette (or small container)

Artification tools

Magic Folder

I expressly encourage you to keep the papers you'll be creating from the exercises in this book, as you may draw inspiration from them for years to come. To help keep them stored in a fun and respectful way, I've provided instructions for creating your own fabric file folder.

You can make this folder as simple or complex as you desire. You may choose just one wonderful fabric, or stitch together a uniquely personal piece of fabric to use, or maybe even utilize an old quilt top or blocks that you stitched for some long-forgotten purpose. The basic construction of the folder remains the same.

Materials

For each folder you'll need the following items.

Freezer paper

Basic sewing supplies (see page 19)

1 fat quarter (18" x 21") of fabric for exterior of folder

1 fat quarter of fabric for interior of folder

2 fat quarters of fabric for interior pockets and closure tab

1½ yards of 22"-wide heavyweight fusible web (I prefer HeatnBond)

14" x 21" piece of Soft and Stable filling for padding between the folder layers

2" piece of 1"-wide hook-and-loop tape for closure tab

2 strips, 2" x 42", of fabric for binding

Natalie Barnes, my good friend and quilting buddy, pulled together some of her favorite fabrics and used flip-and-sew techniques to create this one-of-a-kind folder.

Preparing the Folder Parts

Following the manufacturer's instructions, iron fusible web to the wrong side of the exterior-fabric fat quarter, the interior-fabric fat quarter, and one of the fat quarters for the pocket/closure tab.

Cutting Out the Pieces

Enlarge the pattern on page 17 by 250%, or draw it using a ruler and the provided dimensions to make a full-sized pattern. Then make full-sized freezer-paper patterns for each of the folder pieces and each side pocket. Iron the freezer-paper patterns onto the appropriate fabrics listed below, and cut out the pieces.

From the exterior-fabric fat quarter, cut:
1 folder piece, prepared with fusible web

From the interior-fabric fat quarter, cut:
1 folder piece, prepared with fusible web

From the pocket-fabric fat quarters, cut:
2 pocket pieces, prepared with fusible web
2 pocket pieces (without fusible web)
1 rectangle, 2½" x 6", prepared with fusible web
1 rectangle, 2½" x 6" (without fusible web)

Stitching Everything Together

1. Remove the paper backing from the prepared pockets and the prepared 2½" x 6" rectangle. Place a second fabric of the same shape wrong side down onto the exposed fusible side of each piece. Iron the fabrics in place. If desired, use scissors to slightly round the ends of the 2½" x 6" rectangle to complete the closure tab.

2. Lay the Soft and Stable filling on the ironing board.

3. Remove the backing paper from the exterior fabric and place it right side up on the filling; iron in place. If you wish to quilt the outside panel, this would be the best time.

4. Remove the backing paper from the interior fabric and place it right side up on the other side of the filling; iron in place.

5. Sewing through all of the layers, stitch three parallel lines ¼" apart along the center as indicated on the pattern.

6. Place one part of the hook-and-loop tape onto the back of the closure tab. On the outside of the folder, center the tab on one short end, near the edge of the folder. One tab end should be about ¾" from the edge, with the other end extending beyond the edge. Stitch the tab in place. Then, close the folder and wrap the tab around the folder. Position the other part of the tape on the outside of the folder, underneath the tab. Stitch the piece in place.

7. With the interior of the folder facing up, pin the pockets in place as indicated on the pattern. If desired, use scissors to slightly round the corners of the folder.

8. Stitch the two binding strips together end to end, making a 2" x 84" strip. Fold the strip in half wrong sides together and press to make a 1"-wide folded binding strip.

9. Open the folder to lie flat and pin the tab out of the way. On the exterior of the folder, stitch the prepared binding around the entire edge, sewing through all of the folder parts. Fold the binding to the inside of the folder and hand stitch in place. Refer to "Standard Binding" on page 93 for detailed instructions as needed.

Sew the binding to the outside of the folder.

I asked some of my quilting friends to make up folders of their own. Look for the impressive results in each of the design basic sections throughout this book.

Folders of quiltmakers, from left to right:
(top row) Jake Finch, Joanell Connolly, Rose Hughes, and Sam Hunter
(bottom row) Karen Gray, Jeanette Kelly, and Vicki Tymczyszyn

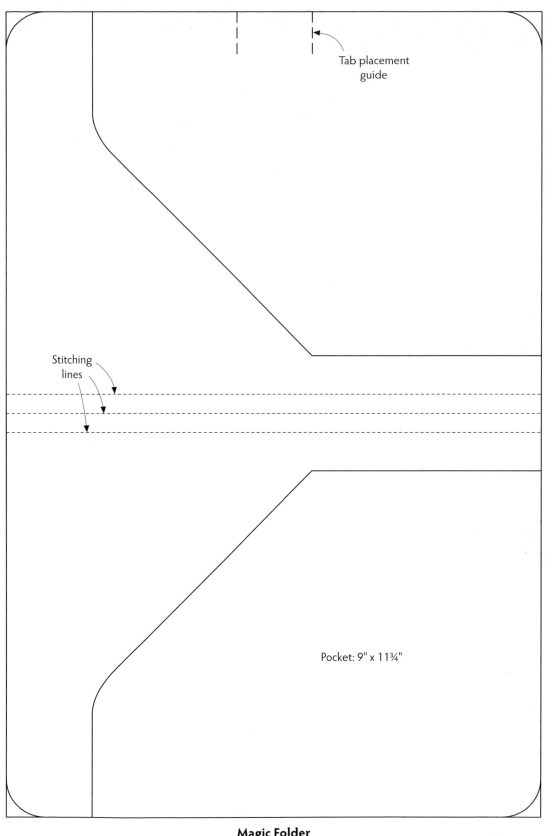

Tab placement
guide

Stitching
lines

Pocket: 9" x 11¾"

Magic Folder
Enlarge pattern 250%.
Overall size: 21" x 14"

Let's Quiltify with the Expanding Toolbox

Quilting for me is magical. There is an amazing transformation that takes place when we throw together fabric, thread, and needles. Add a bit of batting into the mix and—voilà—a quilt of wonderful colors with magical, beautiful stitches and an amazingly simple, or amazingly complex, pattern appears.

This may be oversimplifying the quiltmaking process a bit, but there is magic in it—a magic that comes from the choices we make when we select those basic materials, and even more magic in the techniques we choose when we decide how to stitch them together.

In the years I've been quilting, various styles, techniques, and tools have fallen in and out of favor with quilters, but quilters always have a similar goal. Quilters want to make the magic happen, and we work this magic by encouraging each other, reassuring, bracing up, even emboldening new and old quiltmakers alike. Yes, these styles, techniques, and tools fortify, or as I would like to think of it, *quiltify* us all as we work our own magic.

There are tools that make us all quilters—fabric, thread, needles, batting—and tools that help us keep the magic growing.

Tools That Make Us Quilters

Your projects will flow together smoothly when you use the proper tools and supplies for the job. While I don't know the magic words to make projects suddenly appear completed, I can tell you that the old adage about using the right tool for the job applies to quilters as it does to all crafters. The following information will guide your tool selection.

FABRIC

Traditional cottons used in our quilts are available in many colors, textures, and fun prints—deciding which to use is the hardest part. Add in the possibility of luscious silks and other nontraditional fabrics, and the decision making gets even more complex. In "Opening Up to the World of Color" on page 55, you'll find information on selecting colors and how to choose fabrics that help create the right mood. Keep in mind that for fabrics other than cotton, you'll want to make sure they can be ironed without incident before using them in these projects. All silks and other fabrics that may fray must be stabilized by applying a light to sheer iron-on interfacing. I press interfacing onto the full length of these fabrics prior to cutting them to size.

QUILTIFY

quil•ti•fy (verb)

1. strengthen quilt skills by learning the basic quilt methods and increasing your knowledge by learning new techniques as they become available

2. apply knowledge of basic art elements and design principles to quilt projects

3. encourage others and share ideas with fresh new visions

BASIC SEWING KIT

Here's a complete list of the essentials needed to make the wonderful quilts in this book.

For Drawing and Marking

- Soft-lead pencil
- Pencil eraser
- Fine-line (*not* ultrafine) permanent black marker
- Blunt-ended pencil-like tool (my favorite is a wooden knitting needle)
- Tracing paper
- Cartridge-type chalk powder marker (optional)
- Fabric markers (optional)
- Freezer Paper

For Cutting

- Paper scissors
- Fabric scissors
- Duckbill appliqué scissors
- Rotary cutter and cutting mat
- Long ruler

For Machine Sewing

- Size 80/12 or 90/14 topstitching or metallic sewing-machine needles
- Size 100/16 topstitching sewing-machine needles for 12-weight wool thread

For Pressing

- Iron
- Ironing board
- Pressing sheet (to protect ironing surfaces when using fusible products)

For Basting

- Lightweight-cotton or cotton-blend batting
- Masking tape
- Safety pins

For Dimensional Stitching and Beading

- Size 2 crewel hand-sewing needles
- Size 10 or 11 Sharp hand-sewing needles
- Needle threader (optional)
- Thimble (optional)
- Small pin cushion
- Beading cup or tray

SEWING MACHINE

For the projects in this book, you should use a sewing machine that you're familiar with and that has zigzag and machine-quilting capability. Be sure it's in good working order and that you know how to change the length and width of the stitches.

SEWING-MACHINE FEET. Besides a standard or ¼" foot for straight stitching, you'll need a foot that accommodates wide zigzag stitching. Most machines come with a foot that has an open area for the needle to move back and forth for the zigzag stitch, but since we'll be using this foot to couch over yarns, there are better choices available for most machines. Check with your sewing-machine manufacturer for a foot designed to couch yarn easily. You may also want to have a darning or quilting foot available for optional free-motion machine quilting.

SEWING THREAD. Use a mid-weight cotton thread in a neutral color, such as gray or beige. The best color choice would be one that is visible from the top but not high in contrast. Use this thread for the top and in the bobbin while sewing the pieces of the quilt top together.

QUILTING THREAD. The quilting stitch has a big role in the final look of your piece, and choosing a great thread is the first step. The thickness and quality of the line should be considered. There are shiny, beautiful metallic options, and thicker wool options that are wonderful to use. Silks or other decorative threads that coordinate with chosen yarns for couching and quilting are great choices, too. Mix them up, it's fun!

Here's a collection of some of my favorite machine-quilting threads. Amazing choices are available today, so give them a try!

BOBBIN THREAD. When selecting bobbin thread for couching and quilting, select one that will work well with the backing fabric. Remember, this thread will show on the back of the quilt. In most cases my personal choice is clear monofilament, but I use this thread only in a metal bobbin filled no more than halfway for consistent results.

INTERFACING

When you are using silk or another fabric that frays easily, or you merely need to give a project a bit more shape and support, interfacing is your friend. It has been used in garment construction for a long time, customarily as an extra textile layer in collars, cuffs, necklines, and pockets. There are two basic types, sew-in and fusible, and for our use, fusible is the best choice.

Interfacing comes in a variety of weights and degrees of stiffness to suit different purposes. A very light-weight interfacing works well on silk to set the yarns so they won't fray. Pellon 845 is currently my favorite for using with silk.

Once you have selected the best weight of interfacing for your silk project or other purpose, follow the manufacturer's instructions to iron the interfacing to the wrong side of the fabric, prior to cutting out the pattern pieces for your quilt.

Tools That Lift the Lid on Possibilities

While fabric, thread, and needles bring us together, there are always new tools and techniques that let us express our individuality. These special, fun materials and gadgets are out there for the taking, like toys in a giant toy chest waiting to be pulled out, explored, and played with.

Let's crack open the lid and pull out some of the yarn, beads, and embroidery threads that are near the top. Then be ready to lift the lid of that toy chest higher, reach in for some special tools, and learn how to quiltify with them, endeavoring always to create an assortment of new possibilities.

AUDITIONING YARN

Thickness, color, and texture are areas to consider when selecting yarns for your projects, but the most important thing is to have fun. Jump in and have a great time visiting your local yarn stores, swapping bits of yarns with friends, and enjoying this new source of inspiration.

There is an amazing array of yarns to discover and try, but keep a couple things in mind while searching for the perfect yarn for your quilt. First and foremost, go for color, and in the same way that you select your fabrics, lay out the yarn on the quilt top during your selection process.

You'll also want to consider the thickness and texture of the yarn. Some might be too thin, and some might be too thick—you'll need to find the one that is just right. When used on a quilt, yarn that is too thin may not give you adequate coverage. The solution is to combine multiple strands, which also gives you a chance to mix various textures.

Combining several different yarns along with specialty threads can add color and texture to a quilt while creating thickness for good coverage.

Thicker yarns may cover well, but extra-thick yarns can be difficult to stitch. They can create pulling or bunching as you sew, or your sewing machine may not provide a stitch wide enough to successfully couch down the really thick yarns. If this happens, it's better to select another option.

BEADS

Beading is like accessorizing a favorite wild, night-on-the-town outfit. And, just like the choices you have with fashion, there are endless options for embellishing your quilt. Beads are a great place to start. Beads are available in almost any and every substance—glass, wood, stone, and ceramics, to name a few. They can be of natural or man-made materials, and they come in every shape and size, plus every color of the rainbow.

Beads are fun. In my "gold" stash I have beads made from glass, stone, ceramics, and shell.

When selecting beads, it's important to consider how they will lie on your quilt; large, bulky beads will create a big bump in your work and keep it from lying flat. Don't worry, though, because there are loads of beads out there that will lie flat on your quilt. You can find them by canvassing your local bead stores, checking out bead retailers when traveling, or browsing the Internet.

Two of my favorite beads are commonly available. Bugle beads have a tubular shape and add sparkle, dimension, and direction to a piece. Seed beads are round and can add sparkle, dimension, and texture. Mixing them together makes it easy and fun to create depth and interest within your quilt.

Beads may be strung or sewn from different directions. Notice how the bead is strung when you make your selection. The location of the holes will determine the direction in which the bead will lie on the quilt.

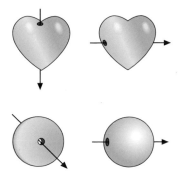

Beads may be strung or sewn from different directions. Each effects how the beads may appear so watch for how the bead is strung as you make your selection.

BEADING THREAD

When beading by hand, use an exceptionally strong but pliable thread in colors that match the fabric colors where the beads will be sewn. My favorite beading thread is 60-weight lint-free polyester (Bottom Line by Superior Threads).

PEARL COTTON AND EMBROIDERY FLOSS

Think big, dimensional stitching!

EMBROIDERY FLOSS. This decorative thread used for dimensional stitching is composed of six very loosely twisted strands, making it highly versatile. The six strands can be used together as they come off the skein, or you can easily separate them into any number of strands. Separated or joined with other colors, strands of floss help to create special effects. Embroidery floss is generally available by the skein, in cotton, silk, and rayon, and can be found in a wide range of colors including some variegated types.

PEARL COTTON. This is another type of decorative thread that may be used for dimensional stitching, but unlike embroidery floss, it's tightly twisted and is not divisible. It's smooth with a low luster, highly praised for strength and durability, and is available in a huge variety of weights and colors. Pearl cotton is generally available for purchase in either skeins or balls. The most common sizes are 12, which is very fine; 8, which is fine; 5, which is medium; and 3, which is heavy.

So many beautiful threads, ready to be needled up and stitched into your next quilting project

Needles Threaded, Ready for Bead and Big-Stitch Quilting

I love hand work and the exquisite line that hand quilting brings to a quilt, but early on I found that I wanted to hand quilt with colored thread. I even hand quilted a couple projects with metallic thread. Then, like a flash, I discovered that I could combine a love of embroidery with hand quilting and use this technique on my quilts.

Embroidery and beading offer amazing opportunities to mix things up even further while having fun. You can turn wonderful, tiny quilting stitches into big, beautiful hand-stitched lines and blur the rules. I use basic straight stitches in a variety of ways, and then intersperse beads throughout in order to add texture and color to my quilts. Now, my quilts just don't seem finished without these additional elements, so get your needles threaded and dive in!

BEAD QUILTING BY HAND

Beads invite your viewers in for a closer look. Here you'll find instructions for my basic bead quilting. The method I use for attaching beads by hand lets the bead be a decorative element while simultaneously acting as a quilting stitch to help stabilize the quilt. The starting and finishing stitches are essential for securing each type of bead.

Starting Stitch

When adding beads to your project, execute these steps every time you begin with a newly threaded needle.

1. Thread the needle and knot the ends together. Insert the needle into the top of the quilt, about 1" from where you want to place the first bead. Continue through the batting and come out through the top of the quilt at the selected starting place.

2. Pull the knot through the quilt top and into the batting layer.

3. With the thread pulled slightly taut, take a single, tiny stitch in place through all three layers (top, batting, and backing).

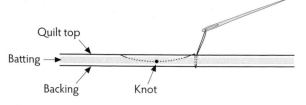

Quilt top
Batting
Backing
Knot

Basic Beading Stitch

This method of beading is very versatile. Just like the seed stitch described on page 23, it lets you fill a surface area, creating either a light or dense covering as needed. The beads can be worked uniformly or randomly, and choosing beads that vary in color, shape, or size can create many of nature's textures.

1. Make a starting stitch.

2. Pick up one bead on the needle and let it slide onto the thread.

3. With the bead on the thread, insert the needle back into the same hole the thread is emerging from and into the batting layer. Push the needle sideways through the batting and up through the quilt top at the next spot you want to add a bead. This is called traveling.

4. Repeat steps 2 and 3 until the last bead has been added or you need to rethread your needle. End with a finishing stitch (below).

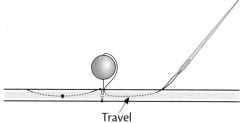

Travel

Finishing Stitch

Follow these steps every time you finish adding beads to a given area and need to end your thread.

1. Bring the threaded needle straight down through all three layers to the back of the quilt.

2. On the back, take a tiny stitch through the backing only. Now, take a tiny stitch in the opposite direction. Then take one more stitch over the previous stitch, creating a small knot.

3. Create a single small knot on the thread very close to the knot on the backing.

4. Bring the threaded needle through the knot on the backing and into the batting, traveling to a point about 1" from the knot. Bring the needle out through the quilt top and clip the thread. Pull the thread tail back into the batting.

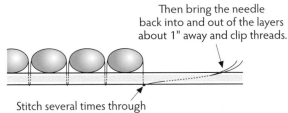

Then bring the needle back into and out of the layers about 1" away and clip threads.

Stitch several times through the same stitch at the back to create a small knot.

BIG-STITCH DIMENSIONAL QUILTING

Big-stitch quilting can be used on its own or in conjunction with couching, machine quilting, or beading. Each method adds its own uniquely special and varying element to your quilt, all the while providing a beautiful way to hold the quilt layers together. You can add color and dimension to your quilts using the basic straight stitch in a big way.

Straight Stitch

This stitch is one of my favorites, because it's one of the easiest and most versatile. It's composed of one single isolated stitch, but the fun begins when it's worked in regular or irregular formations in different lengths and sizes. By working it with threads of varying widths and colors, you'll create more depth.

The stitch is simple. Bring the needle up through the batting and out through the quilt top at A to conceal the knot. Insert the needle at B, and then come out at C to begin the next stitch. Continue, sewing through all of the layers (or the top and batting only). Stitches can be worked in a free manner—uniformly or randomly. The stitches can be long, short, or overlapping.

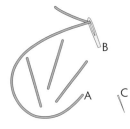

Seed Stitch

Building on the straight stitch, the seed stitch lets you fill large areas with either light or dense covering. Use different threads and colors to create many of nature's textures. The seed stitch is made up of small straight stitches of equal lengths and can be work uniformly or randomly.

Running Stitch

One of the most basic of embroidery stitches, this stitch makes a running line that can be varied easily by working stitches of different widths, lengths, and spacing. Many running lines can be used to build up an area, create texture, and add color.

Work a series of straight stitches from right to left. Bring the needle up through the batting and out through the quilt top at A to conceal the knot. Insert the needle at B, and then come out at C to begin the next stitch, sewing through all the layers.

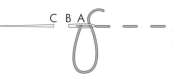

Think of the fun you can have with these simple stitching effects, all made from the humble straight stitch.

Starting at the Beginning—
The Basic Line

When trying to expand your understanding of art, the best place to start is with the most basic element of all—the line. Quite simply, a *line* is defined as a mark that spans a distance between two points. Lines we're most aware of are those used to define a shape in two-dimensional work. Lines can also be grouped together to convey forms and textures, and by their very nature lines are invaluable when you want to imply direction.

The types of line include *actual* and *implied*, both of which are important compositional tools. Actual vertical, horizontal, diagonal, and contour directional lines can be employed to point to important features in your design or create perspective. The same effect of leading or directing the path the eye takes within a design may also be achieved with implied lines.

Additionally, varying a line's thickness, length, and direction is a fundamental way an artist uses line to express character, feeling, and situation.

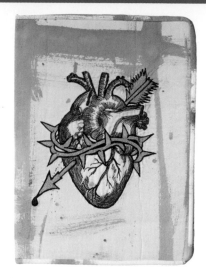

For the cover of her folder, Sam Hunter used thread and only the stitched line to create a heart with incredibly intricate shape and detail.

SKETCH AND STUDY

THE BASIC LINE

For these sketch exercises, you'll need three pieces of paper and something to draw with—a pencil, pen, or markers will all work well.

SKETCH 1:

1. On the first sheet of paper draw two lines, dividing the page into four equal boxes.

2. Mark two dots in each box.

3. Connect each pair of dots in one continuous motion.

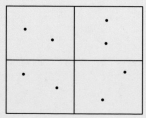

Congratulations! You've drawn lines. Did you end up with straight lines? Or are they wild and curvy? Would you call any of your lines geometric? Or do they all appear organic? Lastly, do the lines you drew all feel the same, or is each one different?

SKETCH 2:

1. Using a new sheet of paper, divide it into four equal boxes as before. Mark two dots in each box.

2. This time, connect each pair of dots using lines of varying thicknesses.

Do these lines look different from those in sketch 1? Do those differences convey different feelings than the lines in sketch 1?

SKETCH 3:

1. Once again, divide a new sheet of paper into four equal boxes.

2. This time, using just lines, draw examples that express the following: *joy, anger, hairy,* and *bristly*.

I believe that through this last exercise you'll have discovered an idea or two that may be worked into your next creative quiltified project.

Winter Mountains

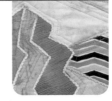

When I think of line, my mind immediately thinks of curvy, wavy, fun lines, probably because of how much I love the great outdoors. In nature there don't seem to be as many sharp, geometric lines as there are curves and winding trails. As I designed this project, I chose to look to nature. I closed my eyes and hiked through the hills in my mind . . . gentle hills, one rolling into the next, followed by another and another, farther and farther away. The trees nearby are larger than those off in the distance, but everything is receding toward the horizon where the hills and sky meet, making it hard to tell where the hills end and the sky begins. In my mind it was a cool winter's day. Close your eyes and try it. Did you imagine a winter's day, or was it springtime?

Once I had this vision in mind, I decided to replace the flowing organic lines with ones that were more geometric in appearance. Just by changing the type of lines, the design transforms from a realistic representation of a hike through the hills to an image with a personal, expressive quality.

Materials

Yardage is based on 42"-wide fabric. Refer to "Fast-Piece Appliqué Basics" on page 87 to prepare the patterns, cut out the fabrics, and construct the quilt top.

Fabric	Pattern Pieces
1 yard of medium-value gray-and-teal cotton fabric	5, 9, 25, 28, 29, 47
7/8 yard of speckled light-value gray-and-teal cotton fabric	3, 21, 23
3/4 yard of teal-blue-green silk fabric	2, 13, 20, 22, 46
5/8 yard of teal-blue-green striped cotton fabric	6, 7, 26, 27
1/2 yard of mottled light-gray cotton fabric	1, 8, 24
1/2 yard of light-pink transparent silk fabric	Sheer additions
1/4 yard of medium-value solid-gray cotton fabric	30, 31, 32
3/8 yard of medium-scale light-blue cotton print	11, 14, 17, 33, 39, 42
1/4 yard of medium-scale ocean-green cotton print	10, 18, 35
1/4 yard of small-scale blue-and-bright-green cotton print	12, 15, 19, 40
1/4 yard of medium-scale bright-green cotton print	34, 36, 44
1/4 yard of textured teal-blue-green silk fabric	16, 37, 41, 43
1/8 yard of medium-scale pale-teal-and-gray cotton print	4
1/8 yard of medium-scale light-blue cotton print	38, 45
5/8 yard of fabric for binding	
1 1/3 yards of fabric for backing	
40" x 43" piece of batting	

Finished size: 36" x 39"

Preparing the Patterns

1. Enlarge the pattern on page 29 to 36" x 39".

2. Use the full-sized tracing-paper pattern as your placement guide.

3. Cut three 18" x 36" pieces of freezer paper. Join the pieces and trim to the same size as your placement guide. Use the placement guide to make a freezer-paper pattern.

Cutting Out the Fabric Pieces

1. Refer to the materials list and use masking tape to mark each fabric with the appropriate pattern piece number.

2. Cut apart the freezer-paper pattern and iron each template to the appropriate fabric. Cut out each piece ½" larger than the template, as shown on page 89.

3. Lay the pieces in place on the tracing-paper placement guide.

Assembling the Quilt Top

Trim the excess fabric from the top piece after each seam has been sewn.

1. Sew the pattern pieces together in pairs as follows: 1 to 2, 3 to 4, 5 to 7, 8 to 9, 10 to 11, 13 to 14, 15 to 16, 17 to 18, 19 to 20, 21 to 22, 23 to 24, 25 to 32, 28 to 45, 30 to 38, 31 to 35, 39 to 40, 41 to 42, 43 to 44, and 46 to 47. Set aside 46–47 for the bottom section.

2. Sew the pairs and pieces into sets as follows: pair 1–2 to pair 3–4, pair 5–7 to piece 6, pair 8–9 to piece 12, pair 13–14 to pair 15–16, pair 17–18 to pair 19–20, pair 21–22 to pair 23–24, pair 28–45 to piece 27, pair 30–38 to pair 39–40, pair 31–35 to pair 33–34, and pair 41–42 to pair 43–44.

3. Join the pieces, pairs, and sets as follows: set 8–9–12 to pair 10–11, set 13–16 to set 17–20, set 31–33–35 to pair 36–37, set 30–38–40 to piece 29, and set 41–44 to set 27–28–45.

4. Sew set 29–30–38–40 to set 27–28–41–45, set 1–4 to set 5–7, set 8–12 to set 13–20, and pair 25–32 to set 31–33–37.

5. Sew set 1–7 to set 8–20 to create the top section.

6. Sew set 21–24 to set 25–31–37 and set 27–30 38–45 to piece 26.

7. Sew set 21–25–31–37 to set 26–30–38–45 to create the middle section.

8. Join the top section to the middle section.

9. Join the top-and-middle section to the bottom section to complete the quilt top.

Couching the Seam Lines

Refer to "Couching, Quilting, and Finishing Basics" on page 91 to prepare the quilt sandwich and couch the seam lines with the desired fibers.

Applying Sheer Additions

As a special feature of this quilt, I wanted to add a bit of shiny, fun fabric to represent the glowing spots you see before your eyes as you let the light of the morning sunrise find you. For this effect, I added transparent silk using the following raw-edge appliqué method. Add this type of fabric after the quilt has been sandwiched and quilted so that you have a stable base.

1. Trace the enlarged pattern pieces indicated by the red lines on the pattern (page 29) onto freezer paper.

2. Cut out the freezer-paper pieces on the line. Iron each template to the right side of the sheer fabric. Cut out each fabric piece, leaving approximately 1" outside the template. Do not remove the freezer-paper template.

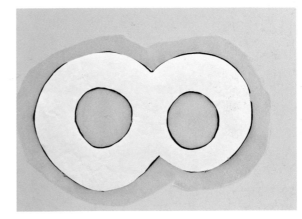

3. Lay each piece on the quilt front as indicated on the pattern. Pin each piece in place.

4. Thread the sewing-machine needle with a decorative thread, and wind the bobbin with a thread that is compatible with the top thread and that will look nice on the back of the quilt. Set your machine for a straight stitch and use a free-motion quilting foot.

5. Stitch completely around each piece three times, sewing along the outside and inside edges of the freezer-paper template.

6. Remove the freezer-paper template. Trim the excess fabric using duckbill appliqué scissors, leaving approximately $\frac{1}{16}$" beyond the stitching line. If you plan to wash the quilt, use a pin to apply a fray-control liquid to the raw edges.

Finishing

1. Refer to "Needles Threaded, Ready for Bead and Big-Stitch Quilting" on page 22 for instructions on dimensional stitching and bead quilting.

2. Attach the binding as described in "Faced Binding" on page 93.

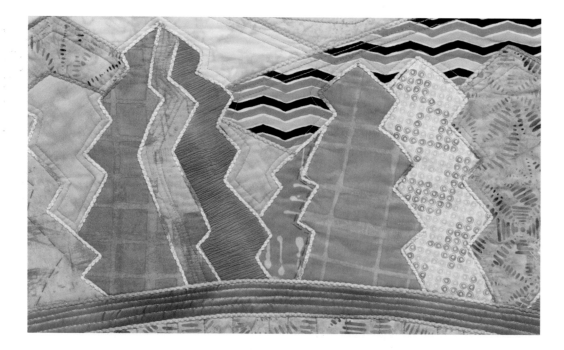

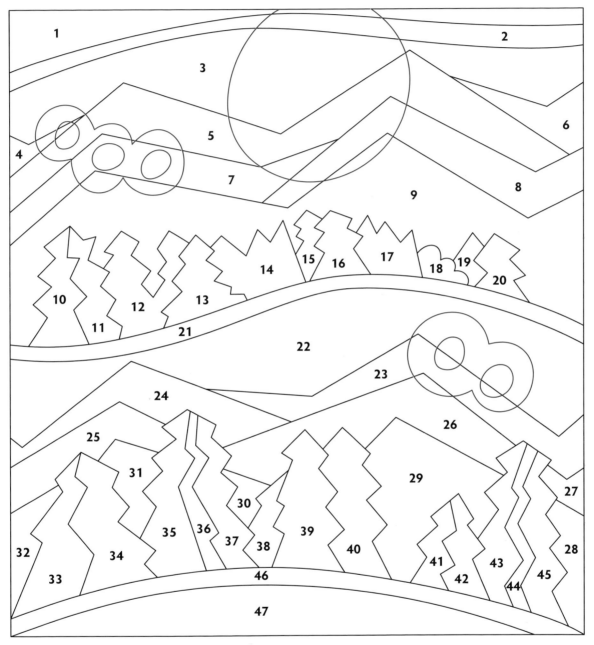

Winter Mountain
Enlarge pattern 600%.
Overall size: 36" x 39"

Finished size: 3½" wide x your waist or hip measurement, not including ties

Silky Winter Sash

Are you on the lookout for something simple to make, that's fun to wear? Something that subtly hints, *I am a quilter?* I'm usually on a quest for just this type of thing, especially around the winter holidays.

This project gives you an opportunity to use Fast-Piece Appliqué to quickly stitch up a fun-to-wear sash that will dress up a basic outfit quite easily. I purposely used several types of silk fabrics for their color and texture, and lined each fabric with interfacing prior to cutting the pattern. There are three basic parts to assemble before the sash is stitched together and it's ready to wear.

Materials

Yardage is based on 42"-wide fabric. Refer to "Fast-Piece Appliqué Basics" on page 87 to prepare the patterns, cut out the fabrics, and construct the quilt top.

Fabric	Pattern Pieces
¼ yard of dark-blue silk print	1, 4, 5, and tie strings
¼ yard of mottled teal-blue-green silk print	2, 10
⅛ yard of textured blue silk fabric	3
⅛ yard of textured periwinkle silk fabric	6, 12, and tie strings
⅛ yard of teal striped silk fabric	7, 8
⅛ yard of textured teal silk fabric	9, 11
½ yard of coordinating cotton fabric	Backing and tie strings
2 yards of sheer or featherweight fusible interfacing	Stabilize silk pattern pieces
1 yard of light- or medium-weight fusible interfacing	Stabilize sash front
4 yards of ¼"-wide coordinating silk ribbon	Tie strings

Preparing the Pattern

1. Measure the waist or hips of the person for whom the sash is being made and subtract 2". Using the resulting measurement, enlarge the pattern on page 33 to that length x 4" wide.

2. Use the full-sized tracing-paper pattern as a placement guide.

3. Use the placement guide to make a freezer-paper pattern.

Cutting Out the Fabric Pieces

1. Refer to the materials list and use masking tape to mark each fabric with the appropriate pattern-piece number. If using silk fabric, iron sheer or featherweight interfacing to the wrong side of each fabric to stabilize the fabric before cutting.

2. Cut apart the freezer-paper pattern and iron each template to the appropriate fabric. Cut out each piece ½" larger than the template as shown on page 89.

3. Lay the pieces in place on the placement guide.

Assembling the Sash Front

Trim the excess fabric from the top piece after each seam has been sewn.

1. Sew the pattern pieces together in pairs as follows: sew 1 to 2, 3 to 4, 5 to 9, 6 to 7, and 10 to 11.

2. Sew the pairs and pieces into sets as follows: pair 1–2 to pair 5–9, pair 3–4 to pair 6–7, and pair 10–11 to piece 12.

3. Join set 1-2-5-9 to set 10-12.

4. Sew piece 8 to the top of the set from step 3.

5. Sew set 3-4-6-7 to the bottom of the set from step 4 to complete the sash front. Press.

6. Cut a piece of light- or medium-weight interfacing the same size as the sash front. Iron the interfacing to the back of the sash front.

7. Select fun, coordinating yarns, and referring to "Setting Up Your Machine for Couching" on page 91, couch the seam lines. Add any additional quilting as desired.

8. Lay the sash front right sides together with the backing fabric and trim them to 4" wide. Trim the length to match the measurement in step 1 of "Preparing the Pattern." Then trim both ends as shown. Do not sew the pieces together.

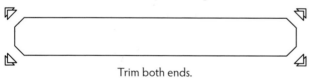

Trim both ends.

Adding the Tie Strings

Each tie string is constructed from two fabrics and intentionally designed to be curvy and fun, with some silky-satin ribbon mixed in.

CUTTING THE TIE STRINGS

1. Divide the waist measurement from step 1 of "Preparing the Pattern" in half to determine the length of the fabric portion of each tie string. For example, if the waist measurement is 30", the fabric length for the tie strings would be 15".

2. Cut four strips from silk fabric, 1½" wide by the length determined in step 1. Repeat to cut four strips from the backing fabric.

3. Cut the silk ribbon into four 36"-long pieces.

CONSTRUCTING THE TIE STRINGS

1. Using a chalk marker or other fabric marker, draw a wavy line on the wrong side of each backing-fabric strip.

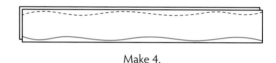

Make 4.

2. Lay one silk-fabric strip right sides together with one backing-fabric strip, pin, and stitch along the marked line. In the same manner, stitch a silk-fabric strip to each of the three remaining backing-fabric strips.

3. Mark a second wavy line on the wrong side of the backing-fabric strips as shown.

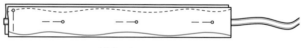

Make 4.

4. Lift the top strip and slide a silk ribbon piece between the strips, centering the ribbon as shown; pin in place. Then stitch the strips together along the second marked line. Make four.

Make 4.

5. On the short end with the ribbon extending a little beyond the end of the strips, sew a slightly arched line. Stitch back and forth two or three times to lock the ribbon in place. Trim along each stitched line, leaving a scant ¼" seam allowance. Repeat with the remaining three tie strings.

6. On each tie string, push the stitched end into the sewn tube; then gently pull the ribbon, turning the tube inside out. After turning, skew the strips so both fabrics are visible, and press.

Finishing the Sash

1. Lay the trimmed sash front on a flat surface, right side up. Place two tie strings, right sides down, on each end of the sash front. Pin and then baste in place.

2. Lay the sash front on a flat surface again, right side up. Pin the tie strings and ribbons in the center of the sash front so that they are out of the way.

3. With right sides together, lay the backing fabric on top of the sash front. Pin along the edges. Straight stitch ¼" from the edge along all sides, making sure to leave approximately 5" open along one long side for turning.

4. Trim the corners and turn the sash right side out, making sure the ties and ribbons are in the proper place and everything is turned well. Press gently.

5. Using a coordinating or matching thread, straight stitch a scant ¹⁄₁₆" around the entire edge of the sash, closing the 5" opening.

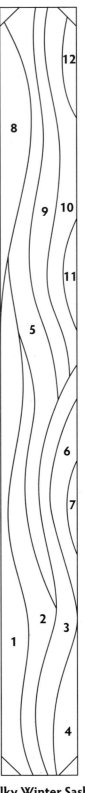

Silky Winter Sash
Enlarge pattern 500%.
Overall size: 4" x waist or hip measurement

It All Starts to Take Shape

Shape is one of the most important elements to quilters. We can hardly avoid it, since whenever we take scissors to fabric and cut, we end up with a shape.

Shape pertains to areas in a two-dimensional space that can be defined by their edges. Think of our rotary cutters making quick work of slicing through those wonderful two-dimensional fabrics, modifying and defining edges with each cut. Once completed, the fabric is transformed; the pieces become self-contained areas representing defined or organic forms, or shapes.

We may be very familiar with the shapes created by the line of our cutting tool, but the edges of a shape may also be defined by color, texture, or value. Generally, shapes such as squares, circles, triangles, and hexagons are defined as geometric. There are also *organic* shapes. These may be irregular and asymmetrical, and they most often occur in nature, such as the shape of clouds, puddles, or leaves.

Shapes also play an important and powerful role in our compositions. When objects are directly placed into our designs, they are known as *positive shapes*. The areas surrounding these shapes create *negative spaces*, and it's the way these positives and negatives interact or interlock with each other that creates a sense of foreground and background. Through their interaction they create a visual sense of space. Therefore, it's important to pay attention to both positive shapes and negative spaces. By understanding these interactions we can make better design choices and more exciting artified quilts.

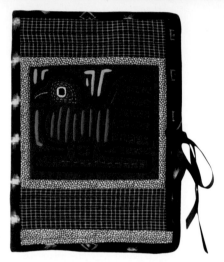

A Mola bird truly takes center stage on Joanell Connelly's folder. Her fabric selection repeats the rectangular outer element of the piece in the center, tying it all together.

SHAPE-UPS!

For the first sketch exercise you'll need a piece of paper and something to draw with—a pencil, pen, or markers will all work well. For the rest of the exercises you'll need two pieces of paper, bits of colored scrap paper or a magazine to cut up, markers or crayons, scissors, and a glue stick.

SKETCH 1

1. On the first sheet of paper draw two lines, dividing the page into four equal boxes.

2. Mark one dot in the first box, two dots in the second box, three dots in the third box, and four dots in the last box.

3. In the box with one dot, start with your pencil on the dot and in one continuous motion create a line that comes to a conclusion where it started, on the dot. You've created a shape. Is yours geometric or organic?

4. In the box with two dots, again start with your pencil on one dot and in a continuous motion create a line that concludes where it started, on the dot. Next, repeat this same motion from the second dot, but do not let your shapes touch each other. At this point, notice what happens to positive shape images in relationship to the negative, non-shape areas.

5. In the box with three dots, again start with your pencil on one dot and in a continuous motion create a line that concludes where it started, on the dot. Repeat on each dot to make a total of three shapes, making an attempt to create organic shapes that intersect with each other.

Note: what happens with your small sketched design and how the positive and negative shapes differ from those in the box with two dots.

6. In the last box with four dots, again start with your pencil on one dot and in a continuous motion create a line that concludes where it started, on the dot. Repeat on each dot to make a total of four shapes. This time, create geometric shapes that intersect with each other. How do these shapes differ from those in the box with three dots?

SKETCH 2

1. Use a new sheet of paper and draw a line to divide it in half.

2. Cut a shape of your choice from some scrap paper.

3. Place your cut shape underneath one section of the paper so you can see the shape's edges from the top. Using a marker or crayon, and the shape as your pattern, use line only to re-create the shape. Repeat this as you like to fill the space.

SKETCH 3

1. For this exercise, you'll use the other half of the paper from sketch 2 and the shape you cut out.

2. This time, place your cut shape underneath one section of the paper, and using a crayon for rubbing, create a textured negative shape while leaving the paper as the positive image. Repeat this as you like to fill the space.

SKETCH 4

1. Cut a large shape from a magazine or colored paper.

2. Cut the large shape into smaller shapes.

3. Lay out all of the smaller shapes on a third sheet of paper and play with the shapes until you are happy with the layout and design. Lastly, glue the pieces in place.

Ideas abound whenever I start playing with shapes. So many quiltified opportunities!

Finished size: 30" x 36"

Mom! Can I Have a Nickel?

While walking through the mall one day, I became intrigued and delighted with the large bank of gumball machines. I just had to pull out my camera and start snapping pictures. There were round and shiny gumballs of every bright color—red, yellow, and green. Then there were the special flavors: watermelon, banana, chocolate, and licorice were just a few of the yummy tastes represented.

We probably all have special memories around these big, round, inviting machines, and most of these memories are punctuated by the words, "Mom, can I please have a nickel?" Or, you may remember asking for a penny. If asked today, you'd better have a quarter handy. You may have been the one asking or the one being asked. No matter, these machines are a bit of Americana old and new, and when it came time to create projects about shape, I couldn't think of a better way to show off circles.

The circles of the machines, the gumballs in all those colors, just had to be made into quilts. In these quilts, I chose to share the idea of gumballs in two very different ways. I started by designing special gumball fabrics and printing them with Spoonflower, an online company specializing in custom-printed fabric.

In this first quilt, I used my gumball fabric and Fast-Piece Appliqué to convey the actual photographs of the machines in fabric!

Materials

Yardage is based on 42"-wide fabric. Fat quarters measure 18" x 21". Refer to "Fast-Pieced Appliqué Basics" on page 87 to prepare the patterns, cut out the fabrics, and construct the quilt top.

Fabric	Pattern Pieces
½ yard of small-scale purple print	7, 8, 9
¼ yard of large-scale black-with-gray print	10, 64
¼ yard of small-scale purple-and-teal wavy-striped print	2
¼ yard of small-scale purple-and-white print	1
2 fat quarters of gumball-machine fabric	4, 6
1 fat quarter of mottled red fabric	3, 5
1 fat quarter of small-scale medium-gray print	13, 16, 19, 22, 25, 49, 52, 54
1 fat quarter of silver-gray print	11, 15, 18, 21, 24, 27, 36, 38, 40, 44, 46, 48, 51, 60, 62
1 fat quarter of mottled light-gray print	28, 29, 34, 37, 58, 61, 65
1 fat quarter of small-scale light-gray print	26, 32, 35, 39, 43, 53, 56, 59, 63
1 fat quarter of small-scale light-gray striped print	14, 17, 30, 31, 42, 55
1 fat eighth of mottled medium-gray print	12, 33, 41, 45, 57
1 fat eighth of solid silver silk-and-cotton-blend fabric	20, 23, 47, 50
⅝ yard of fabric for binding	
1¼ yards of fabric for backing	

34" x 40" piece of batting

Here is a small sampling of the gumball fabrics I created with the help of Spoonflower.

FABRIC DESIGNING

The gumball fabrics I used here are available for sale through Spoonflower. Just go to www.spoonflower.com and click "shop." In the search box at the top of the page, type "gumballs" and then click "search." My fabrics will appear among the results.

You might also enjoy coming up with your own fabric. Spoonflower's website and system for creating one-of-a-kind fabric is easy and fun. I photographed those little round jewels and uploaded the JPEG files following the instructions provided. Maybe the next time you fall in love with some amazing found objects, you'll consider making them into fabric, too!

I opened my Spoonflower account, ordered a sample fabric swatch and a color chart, and I was on my way!

Preparing the Patterns

1. Enlarge the pattern on page 40 to 30" x 36".

2. Use the full-sized tracing-paper pattern as your placement guide.

3. Cut two 18" x 33" pieces of freezer paper. Join the pieces and trim to the same size as your placement guide. Use the placement guide to make a freezer-paper pattern.

Cutting Out the Fabric Pieces

1. Refer to the materials list and use masking tape to mark each fabric with the appropriate pattern-piece number.

2. Cut apart the freezer-paper pattern and iron each template to the appropriate fabric. Cut out each piece ½" larger than the template as shown on page 89.

3. Lay the pieces in place on the tracing-paper placement guide.

Assembling the Quilt Top

Trim the excess fabric from the top piece after each seam has been sewn.

1. Sew the pattern pieces together in pairs as follows: 1 to 2, 3 to 4, 5 to 6, 9 to 10, 11 to 12, 13 to 14, 15 to 16, 17 to 18, 19 to 28, 21 to 26, 22 to 23, 29 to 31, 32 to 33, 34 to 35, 36 to 37, 38 to 39, 40 to 41, 42 to 43, 44 to 45, 48 to 53, 49 to 50, 54 to 55, 56 to 57, 58 to 59, 60 to 61, and 62 to 63.

2. Sew the pairs and pieces into sets as follows: pair 3–4 to pair 5–6, pair 11–12 to pair 13–14, pair 15–16 to pair 17–18, pair 19–28 to piece 30, pair 21–26 to piece 25, pair 22–23 to piece 24, piece 27 to pair 29–31, pair 32–33 to pair 34–35, pair 36–37 to pair 38–39, pair 42–43 to pair 44–45, pair 48–53 to piece 52, pair 49–50 to piece 51, pair 56–57 to pair 58–59, and pair 60–61 to pair 62–63.

3. Sew the pieces, pairs, and sets as follows: pair 1–2 to set 3–6, set 11–14 to set 15–18, set 21–25–26 to set 22–24, set 32–35 to set 36–39, set 42–45 to piece 46, set 48–52–53 to set 49–51, and set 56–59 to set 60–63.

4. Join the pieces, pairs, and sets as follows: pair 9–10 to set 56–63, set 21–26 to set 27–29–31, set 42–46 to piece 47, and set 48–53 to piece 65.

5. Continue sewing the following pairs and sets together: set 21–27–29–31 to set 19–28–30, pair 40–41 to set 42–47, and set 48–52–65 to pair 54–55.

6. For the right machine, sew set 40–47 to set 48–55–65

7. Sew set 40–55–65 to set 9–10–56–63. Then stitch piece 8 in place to complete the right machine.

8. For the left machine, sew piece 20 to set 19–21–31 and set 32–39 to piece 64.

9. Join set 11–18 to set 19–31. Then stitch set 11–31 to set 32–39–64.

10. Sew piece 7 to the set stitched in step 9 to complete the left machine.

11. Sew the left machine to the right machine to complete the bottom section.

12. Sew set 1–6 to the bottom section to complete the quilt top.

Finishing

1. Refer to "Couching, Quilting, and Finishing Basics" on page 91 to prepare the quilt sandwich and couch the seam lines with the desired fibers.

2. Refer to "Needles Threaded, Ready for Bead and Big-Stitch Quilting" on page 22 for instructions on bead quilting and dimensional stitching.

3. Attach the binding as described in "Faced Binding" on page 93.

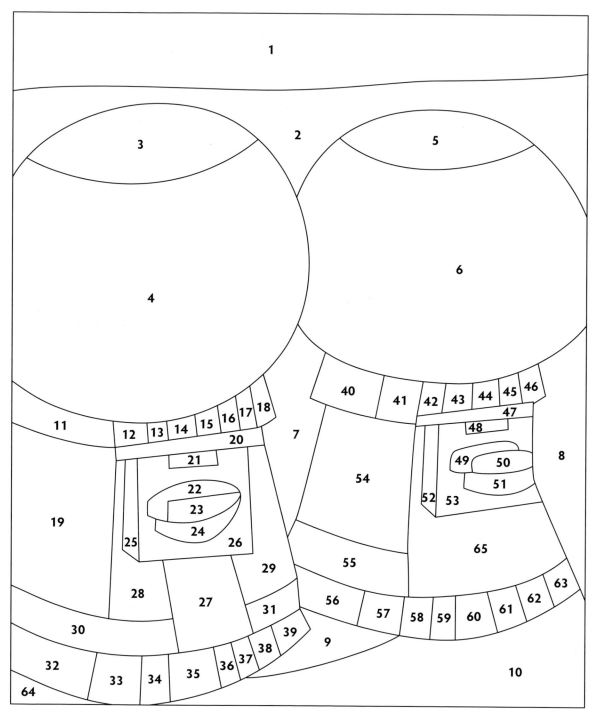

Mom! Can I have a Nickel?
Enlarge pattern 500%.
Overall size: 30" x 36"

Gumball Delight

In this second gumball quilt, I used the gumball fabrics in an entirely different way. The background for this quilt was pieced with a semi-improvisational approach. Then I used Fast-Piece Appliqué to add a colorful, fun layer of gumballs. As in the quilt on page 36, the gumball fabrics started with photographs taken of the real thing. It was fun and easy, but be warned that you end up with quite a few gumballs. Anyone want a sugarless gumball, an apple super-sour, or maybe a mint-chocolate round? Having fun is what making this quilt is all about—and when it's finished, it's large enough to cuddle under while watching a movie.

Materials

Yardage is based on 42"-wide fabric. Refer to "Fast-Piece Appliqué Basics" on page 87 to prepare the patterns, cut out the fabrics, and construct the quilt top.

Fabric	Pattern Pieces
1⅛ yards *each* of 5 assorted mottled light-gray fabrics	Background blocks
4 fat quarters of assorted gumball fabrics	20 gumball circles, 7" diameter
1½ yards of mottled purple fabric	5 curved stripes
½ yard of fabric for binding	
2½ yards of fabric for backing	
53" x 69" piece of batting	

Preparing the Patterns

This quilt mixes things up a bit.

1. Enlarge the block pattern on page 46 to 18" x 18". Use the full-sized pattern to make one freezer-paper or tracing-paper pattern.

2. Enlarge the gumball-row pattern on page 47 to 3¾" x 48½". Use the full-sized pattern to make one freezer-paper pattern. (Since each row of gumballs is the same, you need only one copy of the pattern.)

3. Enlarge the curved stripe pattern on page 47 to 13" x 48½". Use the full-sized pattern to make one freezer-paper pattern.

Cutting Out the Fabric Pieces

1. Cut three 18" x 18" squares from each of the five mottled light-gray fabrics.

2. Arrange the squares into three stacks of five different squares each.

3. Use the freezer-paper pattern as described in "Fold 'n' Cut" on page 43 to cut each stack of squares. Use a rotary cutter and ruler to cut apart each stack on the transferred lines.

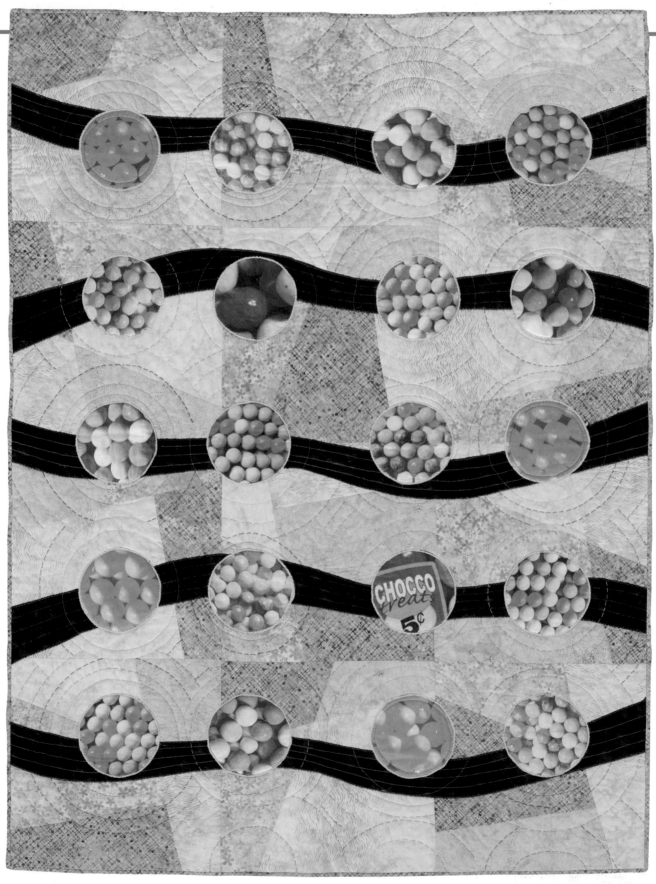

Finished size: 48½" x 64½"

Fold the pattern on a line. Using the folded line as a cutting guide, use a rotary cutter and ruler to cut apart the stacks as shown.

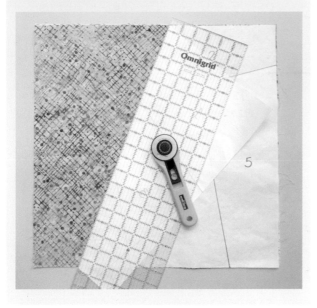

Assembling the Quilt Top

1. Arrange each stack into five blocks, making sure each fabric is used only one time.

2. Place piece 2 on top of piece 1, right sides together and matching the sides to be joined. Sew the pieces together using a ¼" seam allowance and press the seam allowances to one side.

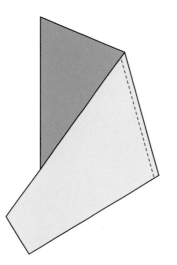

3. Repeat step 2, sewing piece 3 to piece 4.

4. Stitch piece 5 to pair 3–4 to make a set.

5. Trim and even the edges; then join pair 1–2 to set 3–5 to complete the block. Trim the block to measure 16½" x 16½".

6. Repeat steps 2–5 to make a total of 15 blocks.

7. Lay out the blocks in four rows of three blocks each as shown, rearranging the blocks until you are happy with the layout. (Set aside the remaining blocks to use on the back.)

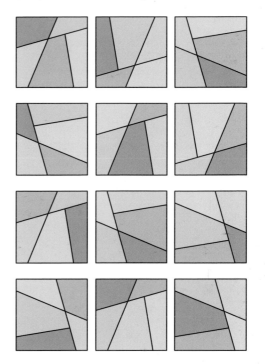

8. Stitch the blocks into rows and press the seam allowances to one side. Then stitch the rows together; press the seam allowances in one direction.

ADDING THE PURPLE STRIPES

Each of the five curved purple stripes is made from the same enlarged freezer-paper pattern.

1. Iron the pattern to the right side of the purple fabric. Cut out the fabric piece, leaving ½" extra around the pattern for seam allowance.

2. Fold the quilt top in half and press with an iron to mark the center line.

3. Using the pressed line as a placement guide and with the freezer paper facing up, lay the purple fabric piece on the right side of the quilt top. Use masking tape to secure it in place.

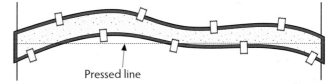

Pressed line

4. Straight stitch along the outer edge of the freezer-paper pattern, removing the tape as you sew. Remove the freezer-paper pattern. Trim the excess fabric close to the stitching line.

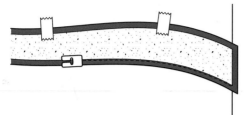

5. Measure up 26½" from the bottom edge and press a guideline. Use this line as a placement guide to position and stitch the next purple stripe in place. Feel free to play with the placement of the stripe before stitching. Trim the excess fabric.

6. For the last stripe on this end of the quilt top, measure 10¾" from the bottom edge and press a guideline. Use this line as a placement guide to position and stitch the next purple stripe in place. Trim the excess fabric.

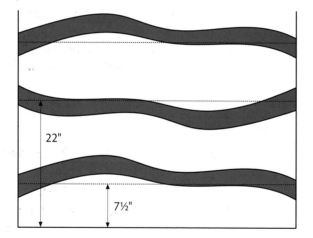

7. Repeating steps 5 and 6, position and stitch two purple stripes on the other end of the quilt top.

SET-IN PIECES MADE EASY

When cutting fabric for a set-in pattern (where one pattern piece is sewn inside another pattern piece), *do not* cut away the fabric from the "base" area where the other pattern piece will be inserted.

To stitch the set-in piece in place, start at the ironing board with both the base and set-in fabrics ready to go.

1. Gently lift the freezer-paper template off of the base fabric until the inner edges of the circle (or shape) are exposed; do not completely remove the template.

2. Slip the set-in piece, right side up, into position on top of the base, making sure the seam allowance of the set-in piece is under the freezer-paper template. Iron the freezer paper back in place.

3. Gently remove the freezer-paper pattern from the set-in piece and press once again.

4. With everything held in place, stitch along the inner edge of the freezer-paper circle.

5. Lift up the freezer-paper template and trim the excess fabric close to the stitching line.

An example of a completed set-in piece

Adding the Gumballs

Each gumball is positioned using a freezer-paper pattern that holds the fabric in place while you stitch. Before starting, make sure the freezer-paper pattern is marked, cut apart, and the 6" circles are cut out. Cut out the gumball circles as indicated in the materials list on page 41, so they are ready to go.

1. Fold the quilt top in half and press as you did before. Line up the pressed line with the center line on the circle #1 freezer-paper pattern. Tack the template in place with an iron.

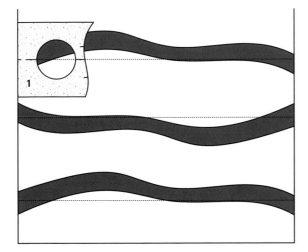

2. Slide one gumball circle in place underneath the cut-out freezer-paper circle, making sure the seam allowance of the fabric circle is under the freezer paper. Press.

3. Straight stitch along the inner edge of the circle.

4. Butt the edges of the circle #2 freezer-paper pattern against the circle #1 pattern, using the hash marks for alignment. Repeating steps 2 and 3, position and stitch a gumball circle in place.

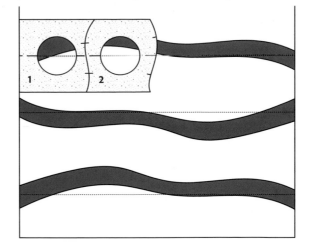

5. Repeat the process to position and stitch circles 3 and 4 in place on the quilt top. Remove the freezer paper and trim the excess fabric close to the stitching line.

6. After the first row of circles is complete, use the same measurements specified in steps 5 and 6 of "Adding the Purple Stripes" to establish lines for placement guides. Position and stitch the remaining rows of gumball circles as shown in the photo on page 42.

Finishing

1. Refer to "Couching, Quilting, and Finishing Basics" on page 91 to prepare the quilt sandwich and couch the seam lines with the desired fibers.

2. Refer to "Needles Threaded, Ready for Bead and Big-Stitch Quilting" on page 22 for instructions on bead quilting and dimensional stitching.

3. Attach the binding as described in "Standard Binding" on page 93.

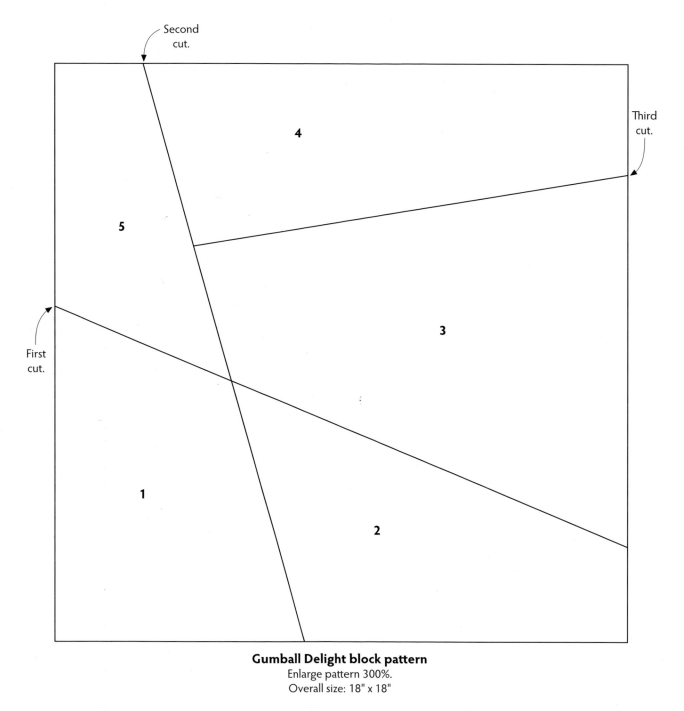

Gumball Delight block pattern
Enlarge pattern 300%.
Overall size: 18" x 18"

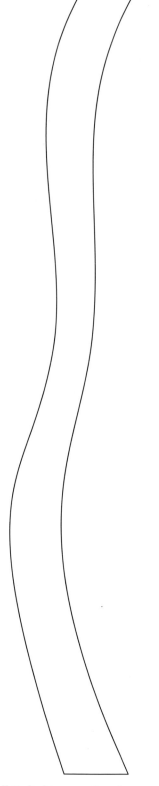

Gumball Delight curved stripe pattern
Enlarge pattern 600%.
Overall size: 3¾" x 48½"

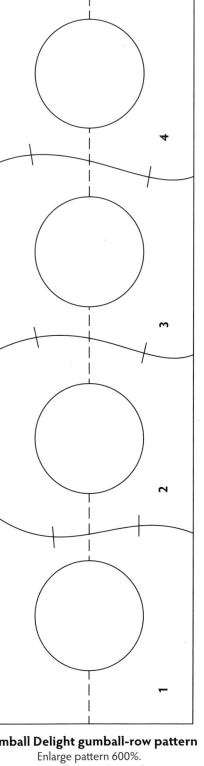

Gumball Delight gumball-row pattern
Enlarge pattern 600%.
Overall size: 13" x 48½"

With a Dash of Texture

At the best of times, we bring a bit of ourselves to our projects as we create. Texture is one of the most powerful design elements for transmitting our personal ideas and surroundings. *Texture* is the surface quality of an object, and words about texture fill our days. We say something is smooth, rough, glossy, coarse, feathery, and on and on, using words to describe the sensations felt as we touch various surfaces around us.

As quilters, we have a very personal relationship with texture. Most of us were drawn to stitching by the wonder of how fabric feels and looks—the qualities that sum up the two types of texture.

Types of Texture—Actual or Implied?

First, there is *actual* or *tactile texture*. As the name implies, *tactile* refers to touch. Tactile texture is the actual three-dimensional feel of a surface or an object.

Second, there is *implied* or *visual texture*, where a two-dimensional piece of art is made to look like a certain texture, but is actually just a smooth piece of paper. It's the visual representation or illusion of a surface's real texture.

Both types of texture are present in quilting. Fabric has a surface and hence an actual texture, but many of our fabrics use patterning to create implied texture and impart additional effectiveness to our quilts.

I've always enjoyed collecting textures. Does this sound a bit strange? For many of you it may not—if you're a fabric lover, you are probably also a collector of textures. Do you remember the first time (the really far-back, first time) that you became truly aware of some fabric object around you? Can you remember how it felt? How would you describe it? Draw it? How would you work that texture into a quilt?

Texture is one of my favorite design tools, and it's important to remember that as we gather more tools at our disposal, and deepen our understanding of how these tools work, we acquire better opportunities to artify our projects. Keep this in mind as you travel through your day. You may just find a texture so intriguing that it turns into an entire artified quilt series.

To expand your understanding of textures, turn to "Back at the Beginning" on page 83, where you'll find ideas about how to continue exploring textural wonders.

Karen Gray used beads and stitching to add excitement to the beautiful fabrics she selected for her crazy-quilt pattern. Each type of bead imparted a new and inviting texture to her folder.

TAKING ON TEXTURES

For these sketch exercises you'll need three pieces of paper and something to draw with—a pencil, pen, or markers will all work well. You'll also need scissors and a glue stick.

SKETCH 1:

1. On the first sheet of paper draw two lines, dividing the page into four equal boxes.

2. Grab your pencil and, with paper in hand, take a walk around your house looking for items that have strong tactile texture.

3. When you find such an item, lay the paper over the object and rub across the paper. This should transfer the texture to your paper. Collect three more, but keep your eyes open for all the possibilities.

SKETCH 2:

1. Using a new sheet of paper, divide it into four equal boxes as before.

2. This time, close your eyes for a moment and think of several things you see every day that have distinct visual texture. These may include bricks, clouds, stones, fabric, tree bark, and wicker baskets.

3. Pick four and draw an example of each texture on your paper.

SKETCH 3

1. Divide a new sheet of paper in half and write "actual textures" at the top of one section and "visual textures" at the top of the other section.

2. Dig through your fabric stash and find examples of both actual and visual textures.

3. Cut a small piece of each of your examples and use a glue stick to affix them in the appropriate section.

Did these short exercises get you thinking about textures? I hope the answer is yes, for textures can be used not only to add interest and appeal to a quilt; these lovely, tactile wonders may also provide the inspiration for an entire design.

Examples of various textures, clockwise from upper left: Aida cloth for counted cross-stitch, coarse sandpaper, mesh screen, mosaic tile, cardboard cup sleeve, and rough stone.

Finished size: 30" x 39"

Textured Kibble Kitty

When it came time to work on creating a quilt to really showcase texture, I looked around my home for an example. As I wandered, my eyes landed on my cat. In this quilt, the cat is made of a hodgepodge of various fabric textures, and I had great fun choosing both tactile and visual samples. That smooth, shiny coat of the cat gains luster with a bit of lovely tactile silk, while those coarse, scruffy calico stripes were easy to portray visually with a variety of batik textures. When it's time for you to stitch your own kitty, I hope you'll include some fun textures of your own.

Materials

Yardage is based on 42"-wide fabric. Fat quarters measure 18" x 21" and fat eighths measure 9" x 21". Refer to "Fast-Piece Appliqué Basics" on page 87 to prepare the patterns, cut out the fabrics, and construct the quilt top.

Fabric	Pattern Pieces
1¼ yards of large-scale multicolored silk fabric	31
1 yard of golden raw-silk fabric	41, 43, 49, 59, 61, 64, 67, 70, 73, 76, 79, 82, 91, 102, 103
½ yard of purple silk fabric	16, 17, 18, 19, 93
½ yard of brown-striped woven fabric	33, 34, 36, 38, 40
½ yard of orange cotton-and-silk-blend fabric	46, 57, 66, 78, 83, 99, 106
½ yard of gold cotton-and-silk-blend fabric	58, 62, 65, 68, 71, 74, 77, 80, 87, 88, 89, 90, 92, 104, 105, 110, 111, 112
1 fat quarter of small-scale brown print	32, 35, 37, 39
1 fat quarter of violet silk fabric	30
1 fat quarter of mottled orange print	42, 47, 60, 69, 81, 85, 95
1 fat quarter of small-scale gold-and-orange print	63, 94, 96, 98, 109
1 fat quarter of small-scale orange print	44, 45, 56, 72, 75, 84, 86, 97, 107, 108
1 fat quarter of textured multicolored silk fabric	48, 100, 101
1 fat quarter of mottled teal silk fabric	3, 8, 14
1 fat quarter of yellow cotton velveteen fabric	1, 6
1 fat quarter of light-blue silk fabric	4, 7, 9, 11, 13
1 fat quarter of teal-blue silk fabric	2, 5, 10, 12
1/8 yard of orange silk fabric	15
1 fat eighth of mottled green print	21, 24
1 fat eighth of mottled dark-green print	22, 25, 28, 29
1 fat eighth of teal-blue-green print	20, 23, 26, 27
Scraps of assorted striped black and purple silk fabrics	50, 51, 52, 53, 54, 55 (eyes)
5/8 yard of fabric for binding	
1⅓ yards of fabric for backing	
34" x 43" piece of batting	

Preparing the Pattern

1. Enlarge the pattern on page 54 to 30" x 39".

2. Use the full-sized tracing-paper pattern as your placement guide.

3. Cut three 18" x 30" pieces of freezer paper. Join the pieces and trim to the same size as your placement guide. Use the placement guide to make a freezer-paper pattern.

Cutting Out the Fabric Pieces

1. Refer to the materials list and use masking tape to mark each fabric with the appropriate pattern-piece number.

2. Cut apart the freezer-paper pattern and iron each template to the appropriate fabric. Cut out each piece ½" larger than the template as shown on page 89.

3. Lay the pieces in place on the tracing-paper placement guide.

Joining the Pieces

This quilt has a lot of pieces. After sewing the pieces into pairs, we'll focus on constructing the various sections. Trim the excess fabric from the top piece after each seam has been sewn.

1. Sew the pattern pieces together in pairs as follows: 1 to 2, 4 to 5, 7 to 8, 9 to 10, 11 to 12, 13 to 14, 21 to 22, 23 to 24, 25 to 26, 27 to 28, 29 to 93, 32 to 33, 35 to 36, 38 to 39, 41 to 42, 43 to 44, 48 to 49, 51 to 52, 54 to 55, 56 to 57, 59 to 60, 61 to 62, 64 to 65, 67 to 68, 70 to 71, 73 to 74, 76 to 77, 79 to 80, 91 to 92, 101 to 102, and 103 to 104.

2. Lay the stiched pairs back onto the tracing-paper placement guide.

Making the Top Section

1. To make the top section, sew the following pairs into sets: pair 7–8 to pair 9–10 and pair 11–12 to pair 13–14.

2. Sew set 7–10 to set 11–14. Then sew piece 6 to set 7–14.

3. Sew pair 1–2 to set 6–14. Then add piece 18 to complete the top section.

Making the Tail Section

1. Sew the pairs and pieces into sets as follows: piece 3 to pair 4–5, pair 61–62 to piece 63, pair 64–65 to piece 66, pair 67–68 to piece 69, pair 70–71 to piece 72, pair 73–74 to piece 75, pair 76–77 to piece 78, and pair 79–80 to piece 81.

2. Sew the pieces, pairs, and sets together as follows: set 3–5 to piece 16, pair 59–60 to set 61–63, set 64–66 to set 67–69, set 70–72 to set 73–75, and set 76–78 to set 79–81.

3. Sew set 59–63 to set 64–69 and set 70–75 to set 76–81.

4. Sew set 59–69 to set 70–81 to create the tail.

5. Sew set 3–5–16 to set 59–81. Then add piece 17 to complete the tail section.

Making the Cat Body

The cat body has many small pieces that are best handled as set-in pieces. Refer to "Set-In Pieces Made Easy" on page 44 as needed. Cut piece 82 as one piece of fabric. In this pattern, a group of pieces will be set in, trimmed, and followed by the next group of set-in pieces. Set the following pieces into piece 82:

Group 1: pieces 94–99

Group 2: pieces 87–90

Group 3: piece 105 and pieces 110–112

Group 4: pieces 83–86

Group 5: pieces 106–109

Making the Cat Face

1. Set pair 41–42 into piece 30. Then set pair 43–44 into piece 30.

2. Set pieces 45, 46, and 47 into pair 48–49 to create set 45–49.

3. Sew set 45–49 to pair 56–57 to create the top section of the face.

4. Sew piece 50 to pair 51–52 and piece 53 to pair 54–55 to create the eyes.

5. Sew set 53–55 to piece 58. Then sew set 50–52 to piece 58 to create the bottom section of the face.

6. Join the top and bottom sections to complete the face.

Assembling the Quilt Top

1. Sew piece 20 to pair 21–22 and pair 23–24 to pair 25–26. Then sew set 23–26 to pair 27–28.

2. Sew set 20–22 to the left side of set 30–41–44. Then sew set 23–28 to the top of this unit to complete the middle section.

3. Join the pieces, pairs, and sets as follows: pair 103–104 to piece 37, pair 32–33 to piece 34, pair 29–93 to pair 91–92, and pair 38–39 to piece 40.

4. Sew set 29–91–93 to pair 35–36. Then sew this set to set 37–103–104.

5. Sew piece 19 to set 32–34. Sew this set to the set from step 4.

6. Sew set 38–40 to the set from step 5 to create the floor section.

7. Sew the cat face to the middle section. Then sew the tail section to the middle section.

8. Sew piece 100 to the cat body section. Then sew pair 101–102 to the cat body section.

9. Sew the cat body to the middle section.

10. Join the cat body/middle section to the floor section.

11. Join the top section to the middle-and-floor sections.

12. Sew piece 15 to the left side and piece 31 to the right side to complete the quilt top.

Finishing

1. Refer to "Couching, Quilting, and Finishing Basics" on page 91 to prepare the quilt sandwich and couch the seam lines with the desired fibers.

2. Refer to "Needles Threaded, Ready for Bead and Big-Stitch Quilting" on page 22 for instructions on bead quilting and dimensional stitching.

3. Attach the binding as described in "Faced Binding" on page 93.

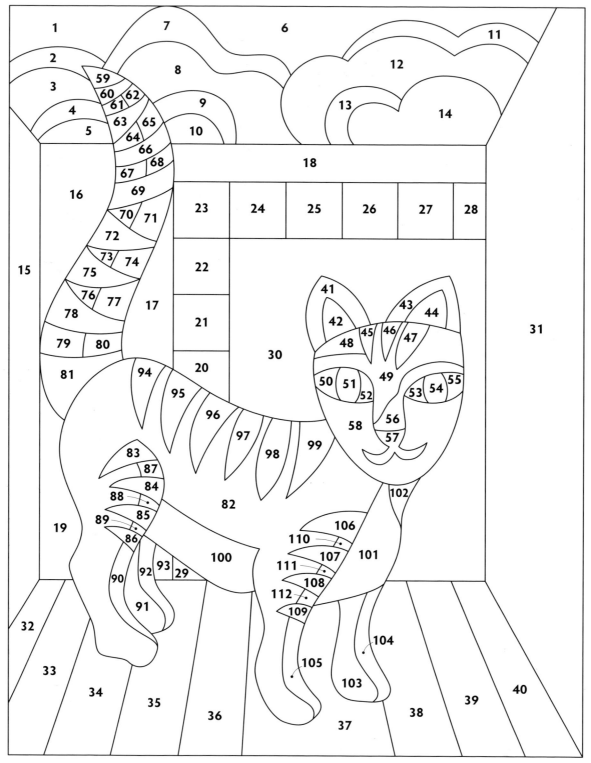

Textured Kibble Kitty
Enlarge pattern 500%.
Overall size: 30" x 39"

Opening Up to the World of Color

Color is an amazing tool for all artists and it's one of the first things to grab our attention. The subject of color—its history, science, and theory—fills bookshelves, and if you do a search for "color" on the Internet, you're likely to get millions of results. As a tool for creating art, color is very important, and yet color is also very personal. The information here is meant to encourage you to enjoy color, learn more about it, and explore ways to use it.

The basic properties and theories of color are always the best place to start. A color wheel, showing the arrangement of colors in a circle, helps us understand basic color relationships. The colors represented on the color wheel are pure, bright colors known as hues. Black and white are not part of that family of hues. White represents the presence of light, and when hues are combined with white they are called tints. Black represents the absence of light, and when hues are combined with black they become shades.

Yellow, red, and blue hues are known as primary colors, and in certain combinations they make up all the other hues on the color wheel.

I'll never misplace this portfolio, and the cool colors will soothe me as I try out all sorts of new ideas. I used an old quilt top that I had never completed, and I'm very pleased with the results.

While painters need a palette of paints, quilters get their color from other sources. Here the primary colors from a color wheel are expressed in threads, yarns, buttons, and beads—all the materials so essential when I start creating.

Secondary colors are created when two of the primary colors are mixed in equal amounts. Green is the mixture of yellow and blue. Violet is a mixture of blue and red, and orange is a mixture of red and yellow. On a color wheel they are exactly midway between each of the primary colors.

Secondary colors expressed in fabrics, yarns, and beads

Tertiary colors are each a mixture of a primary and a secondary color, and you'll find them on the color wheel between their two component colors. There are six tertiary colors: yellow-green, blue-green, blue-violet, red-violet, red-orange, and yellow-orange.

Tertiary colors expressed in fabrics, yarns, and beads

Learning about color theory is important, but observation is the key to really understanding how to use color. Open your eyes to nature and life around you, paying special attention to color. You may be surprised by where color shows up and how just a small amount of color can change the feeling of a whole scene. Observe, experiment for yourself, and you'll soon find wonderful new ways to artify every quilt you make.

Putting aside all the theories about choosing and using color, color is a tool highly worth further study. The more you expose yourself to color, the more you will relish its use and the powerful effect it has in the artification of your quilts. Find more ways to expose yourself to color in "Back at the Beginning" on page 83.

COLOR THEORY TO SUIT THE MOOD

Colors working together help support the mood we want to create and can guide us toward selecting just the right fabrics.

- Greens, blues, and violets are considered cool colors. They tend to recede when viewed and create a calm, serene feeling for the viewer.

- Warm colors such as reds, yellows, and oranges heat things up. They tend to advance toward the viewer and generally are associated with warmth, like the shining sun or a roaring fire.

- A monochromatic scheme uses one color and any tint or shade of the selected color. This generally creates a serene feeling, but doesn't rule out the drama created in the dark shadows of a doorway, or by the bright highlights seen on a sunny afternoon.

- An analogous color scheme creates a beautiful, harmonious feeling by incorporating three colors adjacent to one another on the color wheel. How could they not work well? They are part of the same family and contain a little bit of each other.

- Need a bit of "pop"? Then choose colors opposite each other on the color wheel. These complementary colors can cause sparks to fly.

CALLING UPON COLOR

For these sketch exercises you'll need heavier-weight paper, as we're going to be pulling out the primary-color paints of red, yellow, and blue along with a paintbrush or two. These will be the perfect supplies to use as we begin experiencing and experimenting with color. If you're not familiar with a color wheel, you'll want to have one on hand.

SKETCH 1

1. On the first sheet of paper draw two lines, dividing the page into four equal boxes.

2. In the first box paint a sample of a primary color scheme.

3. In the second box paint a sample of a monochromatic color scheme; in the third box paint a sample of an analogous color scheme; and in the last box paint a sample of a complementary color scheme.

SKETCH 2

1. Divide a new sheet of paper into two equal boxes.

2. Select three or four colors that are next to each other on the color wheel and paint them next to each other in the first box. Then select one color directly across the color wheel from these colors and paint a strip of the new color beside the colors already in place.

3. Use the remaining box to create a scale showing the transition of complementary colors. Select a pair of complementary colors (colors opposite each other on the color wheel) and paint a 2"-wide

band of each color in the box. Using the opposite (or complementary) color of one band of color; apply a small amount of paint on the first color band, creating a new section of color. Continue, this time adding twice as much paint. Keep increasing the amount of paint until you don't have room for any more sections. Then repeat the same process on the second band of color.

Watch what happens to these complements. Each time a color is created, it will work as a neutral for the original pair. These *natural neutrals* can make glowing colors to be added to a quilt. You just have to take the painted sample with you when you go fabric shopping.

Some of my favorite fabrics that represent the colors I found during one of my own natural-neutrals paint trials

Finished size: 32" x 42"

Boogaloo Bungalows

Where do you find inspiration? I find mine all around me—the things I see, the things I hear, and those things that stay with me for years and years. This particular quilt really is a culmination of all those things, but it was especially inspired by songs I heard long, long ago. So much of the music of my youth has visually come alive for me since moving to California, and I have happily turned some of those mental images into the carefree scattering of bungalow dwellings found in this quilt design.

The warm, cheerfully inviting colors selected for this quilt perfectly capture the golden California summer hillsides and the fun, funky boogaloo bungalows. Have the words of your favorite songs ever inspired you to design a quilt? This quilt is stitched together using the straight Fast-Piece Appliqué method. It made easy work of all those wacky bungalows, with their round portals. I hope you give it a try and use this method to create a quilt inspired by the songs of your youth.

Materials

Yardage is based on 42"-wide fabric. Fat quarters measure 18" x 21" and fat eighths measure 9" x 21". Refer to "Fast-Piece Appliqué Basics" on page 87 to prepare the patterns, cut out the fabrics, and construct the quilt top.

Fabric	Pattern Pieces
1 yard of mottled brown-green-rust-and-orange print	1, 14, 33, 48, 71
5/8 yard of textured rust-on-rust fabric	5, 8, 16, 46, 65, 70
1/2 yard of golden-orange silk-and-cotton-blend fabric	3, 11, 20, 31, 45, 56
1/2 yard of gold silk-and-cotton-blend fabric	21, 60, 68
1/2 yard of large-scale green-orange-and-blue print	2, 4, 12, 15, 19, 22, 35, 66, 69
1/2 yard of green-orange-red-and-pink striped fabric	10, 27, 29, 50, 52, 54, 62, 63
1 fat quarter of large-scale pink-red-and-yellow print	6, 30, 32, 55, 57
1 fat quarter of medium-scale red print	7, 9, 25, 36, 38, 40, 49, 51, 61
1 fat quarter of small-scale black-yellow-red-and-orange print	18, 37, 58
1 fat quarter of medium-scale yellow-pink-and-green print	24, 26, 39, 41, 53
1 fat quarter of textured sienna-on-sienna print	13, 23, 28, 34, 43, 59, 64
1 fat eighth of bright-green silk-and-cotton-blend fabric	17, 47, 67
1 fat eighth of red print	42, 44

5/8 yard of fabric for binding

1 3/8 yards of fabric for backing

36" x 46" piece of batting

Preparing the Pattern

1. Enlarge the pattern on page 61 to 32" x 42".

2. Use the full-sized tracing-paper pattern as your placement guide.

3. Cut two 18" x 42" pieces of freezer paper. Join the pieces and trim to the same size as your placement guide. Use the placement guide to make a freezer-paper pattern.

Cutting Out the Fabric Pieces

1. Refer to the materials list and use masking tape to mark each fabric with the appropriate pattern-piece number.

2. Cut apart the freezer-paper pattern and iron each template to the appropriate fabric. Cut out each piece ½" larger than the template as shown on page 89.

3. Lay the pieces in place on the tracing-paper placement guide.

Assembling the Quilt Top

While there are no actual set-in pieces for this quilt, there are some tight circles that may benefit from being treated as set-in pieces. Refer to "Set-In Pieces Made Easy" on page 44 as needed. Trim the excess fabric from the top piece after each seam has been sewn.

1. Sew the pattern pieces together in pairs as follows: 3 to 4, 8 to 9, 10 to 11, 12 to 13, 14 to 15, 16 to 17, 22 to 23, 25 to 26, 28 to 29, 31 to 32, 34 to 35, 37 to 38, 40 to 41, 43 to 44, 46 to 47, 50 to 51, 53 to 54, 56 to 57, 58 to 59, 61 to 62, 63 to 64, 66 to 67, and 69 to 70.

2. Sew the pairs and pieces together into sets as follows: piece 2 to pair 3–4, piece 5 to pair 10–11, piece 7 to pair 8–9, pair 14–15 to piece 19, pair 16–17 to piece 18, piece 21 to pair 22–23, piece 24 to pair 25–26, piece 27 to pair 28–29, piece 30 to pair 31–32, piece 33 to pair 34–35, piece 36 to pair 37–38, piece 39 to pair 40–41, piece 42 to pair 43–44, piece 48 to pair 58–59, piece 49 to pair 50–51, piece 52 to pair 53–54, piece 55 to pair 56–57, piece 60 to pair 61–62, piece 65 to pair 66–67, and piece 68 to pair 69–70.

3. Join the pieces, pairs, and sets as follows: piece 1 to set 2–4, piece 6 to set 7–9, set 5–10–11 to pair 12–13, set 14–15–19 to set 16–18, set 21–23 to set 24–26, set 33–35 to set 36–38, set 42–44 to pair 46–47, set 48–58–59 to set 55–57, set 60–62 to pair 63–64, and set 65–67 to set 68–70.

4. Sew set 5–10–13 to set 6–9 to make a row. Sew this row to set 1–4 to complete the top row.

5. Sew set 14–19 to piece 20 to create row 2. Sew row 2 to the top row to complete the top section.

6. Sew set 21–26 to set 27–29. Then sew set 21–29 to set 30–32 to create row 3.

7. Sew set 33–38 to set 39–41. Then sew set 33–41 to set 42–44–46–47 to create row 4.

8. Sew row 3 to row 4. Sew piece 45 to the bottom of row 4 to complete the middle section.

9. Sew set 48–55–59 to set 52–54. Join set 48–52–59 to set 49–51 to create row 5.

10. Join set 60–64 to the bottom of row 5.

11. Sew set 65–69 to piece 71 to create row 6.

12. Join row 5 to row 6 to complete the bottom section.

13. Join the middle section to the bottom section.

14. Join the top section to the middle-and-bottom section to complete the quilt top.

Finishing

1. Refer to "Couching, Quilting, and Finishing Basics" on page 91 to prepare the quilt sandwich and couch the seam lines with the desired fibers.

2. Refer to "Needles Threaded, Ready for Bead and Big-Stitch Quilting" on page 22 for instructions on bead quilting and dimensional stitching.

3. Attach the binding as described in "Faced Binding" on page 93.

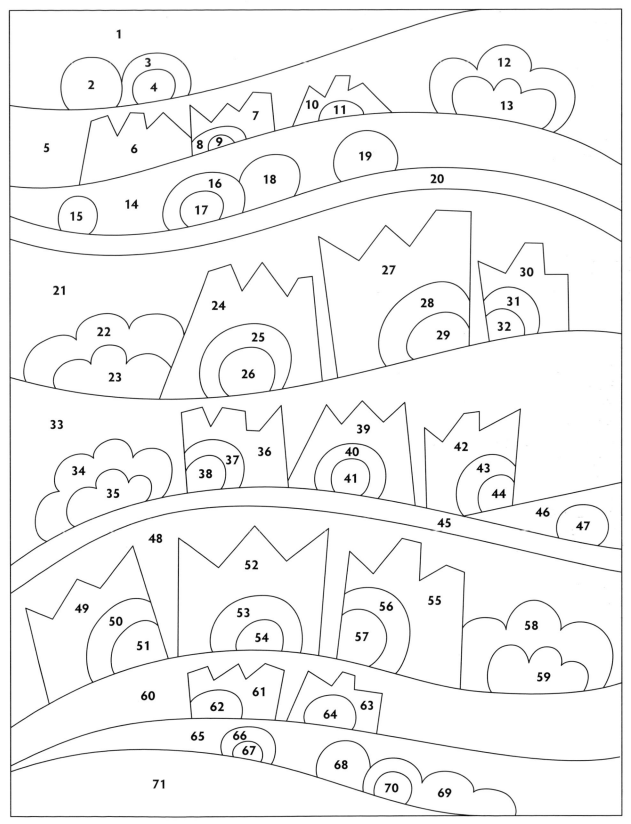

Boogaloo Bungalo
Enlarge pattern 500%.   Overall size: 32" x 42"

Finished size: 41" x 55"

Sand Castles

I grew up close to the Atlantic Ocean beaches, where I spent many summer days playing in the sand and building sand castles. This quilt commemorates those simple little castles with their round towers, and the spirited race with the water that always sought to devour the sand and take it all away. By making the castles in fabric instead of sand, I have a better chance of keeping them for a while. Since this quilt was created to remind me of those long-ago summers, I chose complementary colors of orange and teal blue—calm and warm like those sunny days at the beach.

As in "Gumball Delight" on page 41, you'll improvisationally stitch together fabric pieces to build the background. To create the sand castles, strips of fun orange fabrics are sewn together and then cut and attached to the background using Fast-Piece Appliqué.

Materials

Yardage is based on 42"-wide fabric. Refer to "Fast-Piece Appliqué Basics" on page 87 to prepare the patterns, cut out the fabrics, and construct the quilt top.

Fabric	Used For
⅝ yard *each* of 4 assorted light-blue and pale-teal-blue prints*	Background
½ yard *each* of 3 assorted orange prints*	Castles
½ yard of fabric for binding	
2¾ yards of fabric for backing	
45" x 59" piece of batting	

If the fabric is narrower than 42" after washing and trimming the selvages, you'll need 1⅓ yards of each fabric.

Cutting the Fabric Pieces

From *each* of the assorted light-blue and pale-teal-blue prints, cut:
  1 strip, 18" x 42" (4 total)

From *each* of the assorted orange prints, cut:
  1 strip, 4½" x 42" (3 total)
  2 strips, 3½" x 42" (6 total)

Assembling the Background

1. Sew the light-blue and pale-teal-blue strips together along their long edges, using a ¼" seam allowance. Press the seam allowances of the strip set to one side.

2. Crosscut the strip set into three 14"-wide segments.

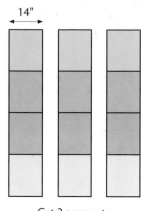

Cut 3 segments,
14" wide.

3. With right sides together, join the short ends of each segment to make three loops.

4. Rotate each loop until you have three fabric sections aligned as desired. Once you've chosen the fabric section you want to use, cut apart each fabric loop to make a 55"-long strip. Make three strips total.

5. Using a ¼" seam allowance, stitch the three strips together along their long edges to create the background of the quilt top. Press the seam allowances to one side.

Preparing the Castle Pattern

1. Enlarge the pattern on page 65 to 41" x 55".

2. Use the full-sized tracing-paper pattern as your placement guide.

3. Cut three 18" x 55" pieces of freezer paper. Join the pieces and trim to the same size as your placement guide. Use the placement guide to make a freezer-paper pattern.

Preparing the Castles

1. Divide the orange strips into three groups, each consisting of one 4½"-wide strip and two 3½"-wide strips. Join the strips in each group along their long edges to make three strip sets. Press the seam allowances to one side.

2. Crosscut each strip set into three 14"-wide segments.

Attaching the Castles

Every castle is made from an orange strip-set segment, but each one is different and requires its own freezer-paper pattern. Each castle is set into the background. Refer to "Set-In Pieces Made Easy" on page 44 for detailed instructions.

1. If the freezer-paper castle pattern is one continuous sheet, rough-cut the castles apart, making sure to leave at least 1" to 2" of extra paper around the drawing.

2. Carefully cut out the center of each freezer-paper castle, cutting directly on the line to make nine castle patterns. Cut out the circles and set them aside to use later.

3. Place a castle pattern, shiny side down, on the right side of each orange strip-set segment. Lightly iron the pattern in place. If needed, trim the fabrics so that the outside edge of the freezer paper extends beyond the edge of the fabric.

4. Arrange the castles as you like on the quilt-top background, referring to the diagram for placement guidance.

5. When you are satisfied with the arrangement, iron the freezer-paper pattern in place. Stitch along the inner edge of the freezer-paper pattern. Remove the freezer paper and trim the excess fabric close to the stitching line.

6. To stitch the circles, lay the circle freezer-paper pattern pieces on the castles as shown in the photo on page 62 and press the circles in place.

7. Stitch just outside of the freezer-paper circles.

8. Remove the freezer paper. Trim the excess fabric *inside* the circle close to the stitching line, being careful not to cut the fabric underneath.

CENTER CUT-OUT TRICK

Use a long straight pin to grab a couple of threads of fabric from the center of a circle. Then use duckbill appliqué scissors to snip the fabric right under the pin. This creates a hole into which you can fit your scissors safely, allowing you to trim away the top fabric without cutting through the bottom layer of fabric.

Finishing

1. Refer to "Couching, Quilting, and Finishing Basics" on page 91 to prepare the quilt sandwich and couch the seam lines with the desired fibers.

2. Refer to "Needles Threaded, Ready for Bead and Big-Stitch Quilting" on page 22 for instructions on bead quilting and dimensional stitching.

3. Attach the binding as described in "Standard Binding" on page 93.

Sand Castles
Enlarge pattern 790%.
Overall size: 41" x 55"

Long and Short of Finding the Right Space

When looking at quilts, we sometimes talk of simple, strong graphic designs. We seldom talk of the perspective portrayed or the effect that one motif may have in relation to another, but we live in a three-dimensional world of depth. When looking around us, some things seem closer, some farther away, so it's important that as quilters we understand spatial relationships and know ways to suggest the illusion of depth.

Creating the perception of space or depth in two-dimensional art such as quilting is a challenge. It makes us stop and think, and no matter how we choose to depict depth, in the end it can never really be completely presented. The challenge comes about because three-dimensional depth cannot physically exist in two dimensions.

Understanding the following techniques gives us options to meet that challenge and artify our quilts with confidence.

DIMINISHING SCALE. We can show the relative distance of objects believed to be of the same size by changing their sizes. Larger objects appear to be closer, and smaller objects appear farther away.

DIAGONAL LINES. Lines moving toward each other in your composition may also be used as a way to represent diminishing scale. This technique is one of my favorites; I love including pathways leading into and through the hills. The pathway as you step into the composition is wide and inviting, and as it moves into the distance toward the horizon, the lines depicting the pathway narrow.

COLOR. How we perceive colors can help us portray depth, too. Warm colors like red, orange, and yellow appear to be close; dark, cool colors such blue and deep purple seem to recede. Color around us changes as it goes farther and farther from our view, so color is also used to create depth by establishing atmosphere. For example, in a landscape, adding blue will make hills and mountains look more distant (fig. 1).

OVERLAPPING OBJECTS. When one object appears to be in front of another object, we take advantage of one of the strongest indicators to signify distance between objects (fig. 2).

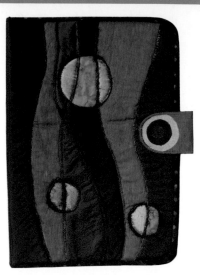

Vicki Tymcyszyn chose to give her folder a sense of space using color and placement. Her complementary color scheme provides just enough pop so that the circles appear to be floating over the background.

Fig. 1

Fig. 2

BOTTOM-TO-TOP PLACEMENT. This takes advantage of the fact that we generally perceive what is at the bottom of a composition to be in front, and what is at the top to be in the back or farther away (fig. 3).

Nature itself can give conflicting signs. Think of how big the full moon looks when it is closest to the horizon. Be open to seeing the space that you are depicting and keep this in mind as you make your own choices.

Whether you're designing a quilt that's realistic, stylized, or abstract, it's important to apply the things you learn along the way about spatial relationships so that you can choose how to portray your ideas. Tools are only valuable if we know how to use them. As our knowledge increases, so do our choices and opportunities for artifying our projects. To learn more about spatial relationships and how they are made two-dimensional in a three-dimensional world, see "Back at the Beginning" on page 83.

Fig. 3

SKETCH AND STUDY

THE ILLUSION OF SPACE

For these exercises you'll need several full-sized sheets of colored paper, scraps of colored paper or a magazine that you may cut up, scissors, and a glue stick.

SKETCH 1:

1. Cut out nine shapes of any size using different sizes and colors of paper for each shape.

2. On one full-sized sheet of paper, paste a row of three shapes about 1" from the bottom edge of the paper.

3. On a second full-sized sheet of paper, paste the remaining shapes anywhere you'd like, but make sure that they overlap.

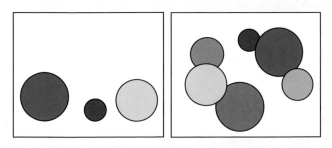

How do these examples differ from one another? What difference, if any, do you see between the two, and which illustrates a sense of three dimensions?

SKETCH 2:

1. Cut out seven circles in graduating sizes, all of the same color.

2. Lay a full-sized sheet of paper in front of you and arrange the circles diagonally across the paper, with the largest circle at the bottom of the paper and the smallest circle at the top. Do the circles appear to be moving back toward an imaginary horizon?

3. Rearrange the circles, starting on the left side of the paper and moving the circles across to the right. Do you see any difference?

4. Try rearranging the circles a few more times, changing the direction and maybe mixing up the sizes. Choose one layout that you feel illustrates a sense of three dimensions, and glue the circles in place.

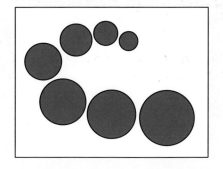

Finished size: 39" x 39"

Tree of Life

When selecting the projects for this section, I went straight to a theme that I have long wanted to convey in fabric. The tree of life, depicted throughout history by artists all over the world and in almost every medium, truly called to me. Did you know that the tree of life is an important symbol in nearly every culture throughout the world? It's interesting, too, that in most of these cultures the tree is shown with its branches reaching into the sky, and its roots deep in the earth. It's said that the tree of life resides in three worlds, linking and uniting heaven, earth, and the underworld. I find the symbolic meaning fascinating and was surprised to learn that it plays a role not only in Jewish and Christian traditions, but also in Norse, Egyptian, Taoist, and even Mayan cultures. The idea of depicting a tree of life in different ways can help us think about how to use the illusion of space in our quilts in various ways. If you enjoy researching and reading about symbolism, I think you'll have a great time exploring this topic more, but only after you give these quilt projects a try.

In this project, I used basic Fast-Piece Appliqué as my main construction method. After reading about the illusion of space and trying the exercises, I think you'll see how this quilt portrays a sense of realistic space by placing the tree of life in the main panel as part of a larger landscape just in front of the hills.

Materials

Yardage is based on 42"-wide fabric. Refer to "Fast-Piece Appliqué Basics" on page 87 to prepare the patterns, cut out the fabrics, and construct the quilt top.

Fabric	Pattern Pieces
1⅛ yards of mottled pale-orange fabric	2
1 yard of small-scale beige print	1, 4
¾ yard of mottled hot-pink print	8, 10
½ yard of small-scale textured light-pink print	7, 9, and 17 leaves
½ yard of large-scale gray floral print	5
½ yard of medium-scale pale-pink-green-and-orange print	3
⅓ yard of small-scale pink-gray-and-orange print	6, and 5 leaves
¾ yard of fabric for binding	
2½ yards of fabric for backing	
43" x 43" piece of batting	
¾ yard of medium-weight fusible web	

Preparing the Patterns

1. Enlarge the pattern on page 71 to 39" x 39".

2. Use the full-sized tracing-paper pattern as your placement guide.

3. Cut three 18" x 40" pieces of freezer paper. Join the pieces and trim to the same size as your placement guide. Use the placement guide to make a freezer-paper pattern without the tree trunk.

4. Make a second freezer-paper pattern of tree trunk pieces 7–10.

Cutting Out the Fabric Pieces

1. Refer to the materials list and use masking tape to mark each fabric with the appropriate pattern-piece number.

2. Cut apart each freezer-paper pattern. Iron each template to the appropriate fabric, keeping in mind that pieces 1–6 are for the background and pieces 7–10 are for the tree trunk. Cut out each piece ½" larger than the template as shown on page 89.

3. Lay the pieces in place on the tracing-paper placement guide.

Assembling the Quilt-Top Background

Trim the excess fabric from the top piece after each seam has been sewn. The fused fabric leaves will be an added embellishment after the couching and quilting is completed.

1. Set piece 1 into piece 2, referring to "Set-In Pieces Made Easy" on page 44 as needed.

2. Sew piece 3 to piece 4. Then sew pair 3–4 to piece 5.

3. Sew pair 1–2 to set 3–5.

4. Sew set 1–5 to piece 6 to complete the background of the quilt top. Remove the freezer-paper pattern and press the quilt top.

Making and Applying the Tree Trunk

After constructing the tree trunk, you will apply the trunk over the background. Trim the excess fabric from the top piece after each seam has been sewn.

1. Sew the tree trunk pattern pieces together in pairs as follows: 7 to 8 and 9 to 10.

2. Sew pair 7–8 to pair 9–10 to create the tree trunk.

3. With the freezer paper still in place, lay the tree trunk on the quilt top where indicated by the pattern. Use tape to hold it in place.

4. Straight stitch along the outside edge of the combined freezer-paper template, removing the tape as you sew.

5. Remove the freezer paper. Trim the excess fabric close to the stitching line.

With the tree trunk in place, stitch around the edge of the template.

Couching the Seam Lines

Refer to "Couching, Quilting, and Finishing Basics" on page 91 to prepare the quilt sandwich and couch the seam lines with the desired fibers before adding the fused leaves.

Fused Leaf Embellishments

1. Use the enlarged pattern to make a freezer-paper template for each leaf.

2. Cut a 5" x 26" piece of light-pink fabric. Fold it in half lengthwise, wrong sides together, and press. Cut a 2½" x 26" piece of fusible web.

3. At the ironing board, open the fabric piece with the wrong side facing up. Align the long edge of the fusible web with the edge of the fabric. Press and let cool.

4. Remove the paper backing from the fusible web. Fold the other half of the fabric on top of the fusible web and press.

5. Place 17 leaf templates, shiny side down, on the right side of the prepared fabric and press.

Freezer-paper template is ironed to the right side of the prepared fabric.

6. Cut out the leaves. Lay them out on the quilt where indicated by the pattern dashed lines and tape in place. Refer to the photo on page 68 as a placement guide.

7. Repeat steps 2–6 using a 5" x 8" piece of pink-gray-and-orange fabric and a 2½" x 8" piece of fusible web to make five leaves.

8. The leaves can be stitched down in any manner you choose. I used a straight stitch and wool thread to attach them with one line of stitching.

Finishing

1. Refer to "Needles Threaded, Ready for Bead and Big-Stitch Quilting" on page 22 for instructions on bead quilting and dimensional stitching.

2. Attach the binding as described in "Faced Binding" on page 93.

Tree of Life
Enlarge pattern 600%.
Overall size: 39" x 39"

Finished size: 42" x 52"

Taking a Stand

The trees in this project make a firm stand while acquiring a sense of stature through the simplicity of their shapes. They stand solidly on the ground and appear to be right next to each other.

As in the project "Tree of Life" (page 69), these trees are made as separate units and applied to the background. This way of using Fast-Piece Appliqué is speedy and effective for adding featured subjects. The quilt is made in three sections—the two trees and the background. Then it's all stitched together and couched the same way as the other projects in this book. With the stitch work made easy, you'll have time to take your own creative stand by artifying the project with wild embellishments.

Materials

Yardage is based on 42"-wide fabric. Refer to "Fast-Piece Appliqué Basics" on page 87 to prepare the patterns, cut out the fabrics, and construct the quilt top.

Fabric	Pattern Pieces		
	Background	Left Tree	Right Tree
2 yards of small-scale light-brown print	2, 6		
2 yards of textured teal-and-gray print	1, 3		
1⅓ yards of small-scale beige-on-beige print	4		
⅓ yard of large-scale beige floral print	5		
⅝ yard of small-scale teal-on-teal print		2, 25	2, 8, 21, 28, 35
⅝ yard large-scale teal-green-blue-and-brown print		1, 7, 14, 21, 24	1, 15, 29, 38
⅝ yard of speckled brown-and-teal print		6, 15, 20	9, 14, 20, 34, 39
⅝ yard of large-scale teal-brown-and-white swirly print		4, 5, 13, 16	3, 4, 10, 16, 19, 27, 30, 33
½ yard of teal silk-and-cotton-blend fabric		9, 11, 17, 22	6, 11, 17, 22, 25, 31, 36
½ yard of small-scale green-on-green print		3, 10, 19	5, 13, 24
½ yard of brown-teal-and-white striped fabric		27, 28	41
½ yard of brown-teal-and-white linear print		8, 12, 18, 23, 26	7, 12, 18, 23, 26, 32, 37, 40, 42
½ yard of fabric for binding			
2¾ yards of fabric for backing			
46" x 56" piece of batting			

Preparing the Pattern

1. Enlarge the pattern on page 75 to 42" x 52".

2. Use the full-sized tracing-paper pattern as your placement guide.

3. Cut three 18" x 42" pieces of freezer paper. Join the pieces and trim to the same size as your placement guide. Use the placement guide to make two freezer-paper patterns. You'll need one pattern for the trees and one pattern for the background.

Pulling It Together with Composition

We use the word *composition* when we speak of creating an orderly, pleasing arrangement of design elements. To guide this process, there are useful principles of design.

In creating a quilt, or any work of art, there is a thought process that takes place. By letting the principles of design guide you, you'll be well on your way to creating a wonderful design in which all of the elements are working together to catch the viewer's interest.

Frequently called the recipe for a good work of art, the design principles combine the elements to create an aesthetic placement of all the things that will produce a good design. When teaching, often my first question for a student is, "What is your focal point?" Many times I can see a student's mind start to whirl—beginning to envision and make choices—and they're off, designing and artifying their quilts. Below is a list of ingredients, all ready to be stirred up.

CENTER OF INTEREST. This is an area that first attracts attention in a composition. It's useful and important to compare this area to other objects or elements in the composition, such as contrast of values, colors, and placement.

BALANCE. In our designs, balance is like visually walking a tightrope. If the balance is off, the feeling just isn't right, and just like the tightrope walker using his arms and legs to stay on the rope, we use shape, form, value, color, and other elements to maintain balance. Balance can be symmetrical and even, but it can also be asymmetrical and uneven.

HARMONY. This principle is used to bring together a composition made of similar units. Think of a quilt or fabric that has wavy lines and organic shapes. Harmony is created by staying with those types of lines. Introducing straight lines or geometric shapes breaks up this harmony and creates discord.

CONTRAST. Using visual discord or separation is equally important. Contrast creates visual differences between shapes. It's used to effectively identify background by bringing shapes or objects forward in a design, creating areas of emphasis.

DIRECTIONAL MOVEMENT. Directing the viewer's eye can be accomplished by using color, value, shape, size, or placement, creating a visual flow along with the suggestion of motion. Directional movement allows you to take the viewer's eyes where you want them to go. As the viewer moves from object to object by way of placement and position, you help to guide the viewer's attention through the design.

RHYTHM. This principle also involves movement, but with some elements that recur regularly. Your composition will have a flow of objects that seem to move and repeat, like the beat of music.

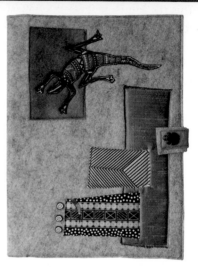

Jeanette Kelly heard about this project and immediately set off to create a very personal folder for her mom. It needed to accommodate a cell phone and an iPad along with a place for paper and pens, so Jeanette made room inside to handle all the gadgets. On the outside she created a lovely composition with carefully selected images from distinctive Australian fabric.

A good knowledge of composition and an understanding of the design principles are essential in producing good artwork. Use them in every quilt you design and you'll be happy with the results. Remember, though, that breaking the rules can provide some exciting results. Some quilters today are bending or ignoring the rules altogether, experimenting with different forms of expression. But when we're prepared with a solid foundation in the rules, we always have a high diving board from which to jump into discovery.

This section provides you with a whole set of principles that act as guidelines to support your further exploration of designing. This information and each of the design-element explanations and exercises are invaluable, but they're meant as a beginning, not an end; I hope you'll take them as an invitation to explore further, to walk on, soak up more, and enjoy it all!

SKETCH AND STUDY

COMPOSITION

These exercises require some paper, lots of pictures from any and all sources you may have, scissors, and a glue stick.

SKETCH 1:

No sketching in this first exercise, just a bit of searching and discovering.

1. The first thing you'll want to do is seek out pictures that you like and pictures that you don't like—the subject doesn't matter. After you find a bunch of pictures, cut them out. Then lay them all out in front of you and sort them into a "like" pile and a "don't like" pile.

2. Working with the "like" pile, and without making any changes to the images, pick one that feels in balance. Glue the picture to a piece of paper and jot down some of the reasons you feel this to be true.

3. Select a picture that you feel has a strong center of interest, one for its harmonious feeling, one that shows strong contrast, and one that has a strong directional sense. After gluing the pictures to separate pieces of paper, record your reasons for your choices.

SKETCH 2:

1. This time work with the "don't like" pile. Select four or five pictures and glue them to separate pieces of paper.

2. Look at each picture closely and determine if the design principles mentioned in this section were followed.

3. Write down where the design principles were followed or where they were not.

4. Lastly, did the handling of the design principles have an effect on why you didn't like these images?

SKETCH 3:

In this exercise, you'll continue using the cut-out pictures, but you'll want to make a simple paper viewfinder from L-shaped brackets. You'll need light-weight cardboard and a thin-line black marker.

1. Cut out two L-shaped pieces from the lightweight cardboard. The short leg of the L should be about 4" long and the long leg about 5". The bracket should be about 1" wide.

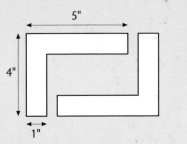

2. Select four or five pictures and glue them to separate pieces of paper. You can work with any of the previously used pictures or select new ones.

3. Use the paper viewfinder to select various portions of the images to create new compositions.

4. After playing with this a bit, use the black marker and enclose your new compositions.

Finished size: 44" x 50"

Along the Redwood Highway

For me there is nothing more special than a cool nighttime walk through the trees. Everything takes on the color of night, and don't ever be fooled into thinking that automatically means black. If we're lucky, there may be a full moon lighting the way or a night sky ablaze with stars. The hills, trees, and sky seem to soak up this warm light and give it back in colors that invite us to walk just a little farther. In this quilt, I hope to inspire that same feeling. It mixes things up by using some traditional construction methods along with my Fast-Piece Appliqué methods, plus design elements that I have enjoyed seeing in many of the works by modern quilters.

This three-panel quilt is composed of one repeated design. The stitching is the same for the left and right panels. In the center panel, the design is rotated slightly. When combined, the intent is to give one the feeling of walking with me through the hills on that moonlit night.

The idea of panels opens up lots of design opportunities. You can make only one panel, make three separate panels so that when they are hung there are three tall tree quilts, or combine the panels into one quilt as I did.

Materials

Yardage is based on 42"-wide fabric. Refer to "Fast-Piece Appliqué Basics" on page 87 to prepare the patterns, cut out the fabrics, and construct the quilt top.

Fabric	Pattern Pieces		
	Left panel	Center panel	Right panel
7/8 yard of mottled red-violet-and-black silk fabric	20, 23	20	22, 23
3/4 yard of mottled brown silk fabric	22	22, 23	20
3/4 yard of textured red-violet silk fabric	21	21	21
5/8 yard of woven blue-and-chartreuse silk fabric	30, 32	26, 29	30, 32
3/4 yard of gold-and-olive-green silk fabric	26, 29, 31	25, 28, 30	26, 29, 31
3/4 yard of dark-blue silk fabric	1	4, 14, 16, 17, 31	1
3/4 yard of speckled dark-blue fabric	4, 14, 16, 17	1	4, 14, 16, 17
3/4 yard of olive-green silk fabric	8, 11	13	12
1 yard of lavender silk fabric	2, 15, 18, 19	5, 15, 18, 19, 32	5, 15, 18, 19
1 fat quarter of mottled teal-and-purple silk fabric	24, 27	–	24, 27
1 fat quarter of teal-blue fabric	25, 28	24, 27	25, 28
1 fat quarter of dark-olive-green silk fabric	10, 12	7, 11	6, 10
1 fat quarter of dark-green silk fabric	7, 13	6, 12	7
1 fat quarter of mottled green-and-blue silk fabric	6, 9	8, 9	11, 13
1 fat quarter of mottled green-and-white fabric	–	10	8, 9
1 fat quarter of pale-lavender fabric	3	2	2
1 fat quarter of medium-value lavender fabric	5	3	3
3/4 yard of fabric for binding			
2 3/4 yards of fabric for backing			
48" x 54" piece of batting			

Preparing the Patterns

1. Enlarge the patterns on page 82 to 15" x 50".

2. Use the full-sized tracing-paper patterns as your placement guides.

3. Cut three 18" x 50" pieces of freezer paper. Trim to the same size as your placement guides. Use the placement guides to make freezer-paper patterns for the left panel, right panel, and center panel.

Cutting Out the Fabric Pieces

1. Refer to the materials list and use masking tape to mark each fabric with the appropriate pattern-piece number.

2. Cut apart each freezer-paper pattern and iron each template to the appropriate fabric. Cut out each piece ½" larger than the template as shown on page 89.

3. Lay the pieces in place on each placement guide.

Assembling the Left Panel

Use the freezer-paper pattern for the left panel and the appropriate fabrics, making sure to trim the excess fabric from the top piece after each seam has been sewn.

1. Sew the pattern pieces together in pairs as follows: 1 to 2, 3 to 4, 6 to 8, 9 to 14, 10 to 16, 11 to 12, 13 to 17, 15 to 24, 25 to 26, 18 to 27, 28 to 29, 20 to 23, 19 to 22, and 31 to 32.

2. Sew the pairs and pieces together into sets as follows: pair 3–4 to piece 5, pair 6–8 to piece 7, pair 11–12 to pair 13–17, pair 15–24 to pair 25–26, pair 18–27 to pair 28–29, pair 19–22 to piece 21, and pair 31–32 to piece 30.

3. Join the pairs and sets as follows: set 3–5 to set 6–8, pair 10–16 to set 11–13–17, set 15–24–26 to pair 20–23, and set 18–27–29 to set 19–21–22.

4. Join the pairs and sets as follows: pair 1–2 to set 3–8, pair 9–14 to set 10–13–17, and set 15–20–23–26 to set 18–19–21–22–27–29.

5. Sew set 1–8 to set 10–16–17 to create the top section.

6. Sew set 15–18–29 to set 30–32 to create the bottom section.

7. Sew the top section to the bottom section to complete the left panel.

Assembling the Right Panel

Using the freezer-paper pattern for the right panel and the appropriate fabrics, repeat all steps of "Assembling the Left Panel" to complete the right panel. Trim the excess fabric from the top piece after each seam has been sewn.

Assembling the Center Panel

1. Sew the pattern pieces together in pairs as follows: 31 to 32, 1 to 2, 3 to 4, 6 to 8, 9 to 14, 10 to 16, 11 to 12, 13 to 17, 15 to 24, 25 to 26, 18 to 27, 28 to 29, 20 to 23, and 19 to 22.

2. Sew the pairs and pieces together into sets as follows: pair 31–32 to pair 1–2, pair 3–4 to piece 5, pair 6–8 to piece 7, pair 9–14 to pair 11–12, pair 10–16 to pair 13–17, pair 15–24 to pair 25–26, pair 18–27 to pair 28–29, and pair 19–22 to piece 21.

3. Join the pairs and sets as follows: set 3–5 to set 6–8, set 9–11–12–14 to set 10–13–16–17, set 15–24–26 to pair 20–23, and set 18–29 to set 19–21–22.

4. Sew set 3–8 to set 9–14–16–17 and set 15–20–23–26 to set 18–19–21–22–27–29.

5. Sew set 31–32–1–2 to set 3–14–16–17 to create the top section.

6. Sew set 15–18–29 to piece 30 to create the bottom section.

7. Sew the top section to the bottom section to complete the center panel.

Assembling the Panels

1. Carefully remove the freezer paper. Square up each panel so that all three panels are the same length and width.

2. Lay out the panels. With right sides together and using a ¼" seam allowance, sew the left and right panels to the center panel to complete the quilt top. Press the seam allowances to one side.

Quilt assembly

Finishing

1. Refer to "Couching, Quilting, and Finishing Basics" on page 91 to prepare the quilt sandwich and couch the seam lines with the desired fibers.

2. Refer to "Needles Threaded, Ready for Bead and Big-Stitch Quilting" on page 22 for instructions on bead quilting and dimensional stitching.

3. Attach the binding as described in "Faced Binding" on page 93.

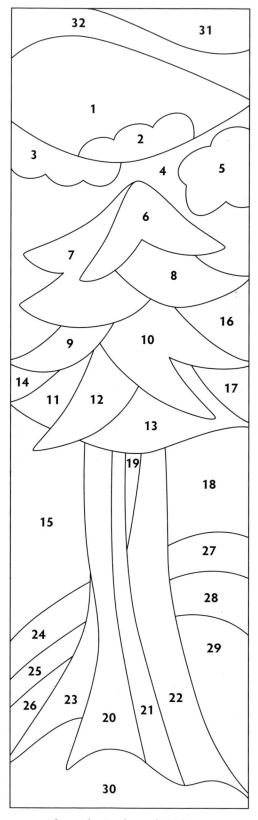

**Along the Redwood Highway
center panel**

Enlarge pattern 600%.   Overall size: 15" x 50"

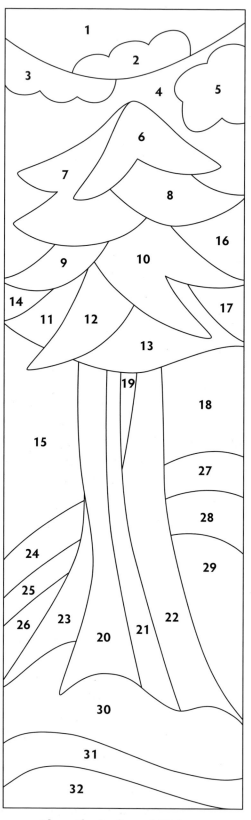

**Along the Redwood Highway
left and right panels**

Enlarge pattern 600%.   Overall size: 15" x 50"

Back at the Beginning

I n this book's introduction, I mentioned how I learned about the creative process and the circular path it always seems to take. As I continue to dive headlong into quilting, this truth becomes clearer. There is a time when you are designing, a time of discovery, and a time when these all lead to more enlightened creating. Sometimes we are doing all three at once, and at other times there doesn't seem to be anything happening.

Where you may be on this path at any given moment doesn't matter, for wherever you are, it's important to take some bits of time to exercise your creativity. Take your art out for a walk and spend time stretching your mind. Throw in a bit of cross-training and time-wasting play (although I don't believe there really is such a thing, since you never know just where or when those *ideas* are going to hit).

Cross-training in our artistic lives enables us to develop new skills that inseminate new ideas and new methods into our art, and also serves to keep us flexible, happily creating for a long, long time. In this section, I'd like to throw out a list of 52 artistic cross-training opportunities, one for each week of the year. It's my hope that you'll find many ideas that will nudge you along and encourage your own personal creative growth. The items listed may pertain to one or many of the design elements in this book—try them. I'm sure you'll be amazed where they lead, while having fun with the process.

Drawing is a key to capturing and experiencing much of the world around you, so it's an important cross-training activity for all of us. Some of you may be reading this and saying, "No, not me, I can't draw," but don't worry. Do this for yourself, and believe that old adage that "practice makes perfect." No matter where you start, you'll just keep getting better and better the more you try, and remember: some of these little drawings may turn into great quilt ideas.

Are you ready to travel new paths to discovery? The list below will get you started.

1. If you don't already carry a notebook (or an iPad) for writing or sketching out your ideas—get one now!

2. Give yourself a month of words. I'm including a list here, and I suggest you write them down on slips of paper and pull one out each day. Make sure you slip in a few of your own as well. Pick a word each day and give yourself just five minutes to explore and draw everything you can think of relating to that word.

   Spacing, density, flow, intersection, separateness, reflection, reticence, integrity, weight, conformity, individuality, timidity, boldness, visibility, randomness, intention, love, animate, instigate, distant, escape, pressure, screw, wind, float, infinity, pairs, organic, original, old

3. Look for lines occurring in nature, and start a collection of the patterns

Here we are, back at the beginning, and Jake Finch's traditionally inspired portfolio seems appropriate. It's a lovely half-square temptress, enticing us all to pick up our pencils and start again. Where shall we go from here?

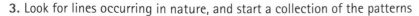

these lines create, either by drawing them on the pages of your notebook or by photographing them.

4. Select 10 words that express various emotions and use a line drawing to denote each of these emotions. Add these to your collection.

5. Select several pieces of music or samples of different styles of music. Listening to these short selections, create a line drawing that denotes each piece of music. Add these to your collection.

6. Use several examples of lines you drew to express various emotions, or other line drawings from your collection, and try to re-create them with hand and/or machine-stitching lines.

7. Pull out a couple of your favorite line drawings along with several fabric markers and ready-to-dye white fabric. Use the markers to re-create and expand on your original line drawings.

8. Look for textures occurring around your home or in nature, and start a collection of these textures, either by drawing or photographing them.

9. You've been on the lookout for visual textures, now sit back, listen, and draw the textures that represent various noises you hear. Add these to your collection.

10. Walk through your home and gather items that have tactile textures. Then place each under a sheet of paper and rub crayons over the top to record the textures.

11. Select some of your crayon rubbings, replace the paper with fabric, and create bits of wildly textured fabric.

12. Select several three-dimensional objects from around your home and create a texture that expresses these objects. Try adding these to your collection first in black and white, and then try creating them in color.

13. Pull out pages from your collected textures, select several, and try creating them with hand and/or machine-stitching lines.

14. Look around your home or studio and find objects that can be used to paint, but no paintbrushes allowed. Try using the found objects to re-create some of the line drawings and/or textures from your collection.

15. Look around at some of the objects that surround you every day. Note their shapes, and take a bit of time to analyze how you might draw them using line and texture. Give it a try and start a collection of these drawings.

16. Tear out various shapes from a variety of colors and then use these to create a portrait.

17. Use the same stacks of torn paper scraps to create a landscape.

18. Using the stacks of torn paper scraps, along with color and shape, create small abstracts that depict *calm*, *nervous*, *floating*, and *stumbling*.

19. Look up architectural styles. Have fun searching through the different types on the Internet; then choose one or two of your favorites and find more examples. How are design elements used in these examples?

Field trips are a great way to get in some cross-training and have fun, too. These trips don't have to be to places far away or require large blocks of time. Here are a few that will probably be very close to home. A digital camera will help you capture all sorts of new and exciting discoveries. Don't leave home without it.

20. Head out to the paint store and spend some time wandering through the paint aisle and all the sample paint chips. Select a few and when you get home, create various color schemes to make your own color samples.

21. While at the grocery store, hunt through the fruits and vegetables for textures.

22. Go to the hardware store, walk the aisles, and make note of everywhere you find the basic design elements of line, shape, texture, and form. Take it a step further by buying a bag of nails or washers. Have fun arranging and rearranging them and enjoying the patterns created.

23. Try the same thing at the gardening store paying special attention to color, texture, and repetition.

24. Take a trip downtown or, if applicable, to the old-town area of your town or city. Note how the design elements show up in the architecture and how the composition may, or may not, take advantage of symmetry, color, line, and texture.

25. Get outdoors. Head to the park. Go for a hike. Bring your sketchbook or your iPad and capture the textures of the clouds. Soak up the surroundings.

26. Go to a museum.

27. Go to an art gallery.

28. Sign up for an art class.

Getting out for field trips, or paying attention to our daily lives in new ways, feeds us with new sights, new sounds, and new ideas to feed the creative cycle. Below are more ideas that may also kick-start your creative cycle.

29. Draw the words from a favorite song.

30. Draw a milestone birthday celebration.

31. Draw a favorite holiday cookie recipe.

32. Draw something inspired by one of the four seasons.

33. Draw one day in the life of your cat, dog, or fish.

34. Draw the fortune from a fortune cookie.

35. Draw your favorite getaway place.

36. Draw your favorite fairy tale.

37. Draw yourself as a tree.

38. Learn about various drawing and/or painting materials.

39. While you're learning about art materials, try some new types of threads. Discover metallic or wool threads and run them through your machine. Start a collection on a test sampler where you can try them out with different needles and on different fabrics for a true test.

40. Select one or more of your drawings and turn them into quilting stitches by marking the drawing on a piece of fabric, then sandwiching this together with batting and a backing fabric, and stitching the design either by machine or by hand.

41. Going back in time can open up new doors of discovery, so choose a period of time that fascinates you, such as the roaring 1920s, the mid-century 1950s, or the counterculture 1960s. Do a bit of research on the clothing, architecture, furniture, or even the cars from that time and soak up all the ways they worked with line, shape, texture, and color. Create a drawing or small quilt based on your findings.

42. In this same way, choose a particular artistic style or period, such as Impressionism, Abstract Expressionism, Surrealism, or Baroque. Pick one that you are not familiar with and that's far outside your comfort zone. Research how the artists of this style or period used the elements and principles of design. Create a drawing or small quilt based on your research.

43. Using as inspiration one of the famous works you discovered during your art-history research, create your own interpretation of the famous work.

44. Flip through the pages of a symbols dictionary; view the images and their hidden meanings. Create a drawing or small quilt based on your favorite symbols.

45. Record your dreams, drawing out the images. Then find a dream dictionary and look up what they mean.

46. Create an autobiographical storyboard. Have fun selecting images that represent who you are and the events that have occurred in your life, and then collage them together. It's enlightening to see the symbols, colors, and images we choose to represent various parts of our existence.

47. Using your storyboard as inspiration, create a drawing or small quilt based on all the images you have collected to represent your life.

48. Gather some leaves, sponge acrylic paints onto the leaves, and press them onto paper using the leaves as you would a rubber stamp.

49. Use unexpected perspectives to inspire art projects. Make an arrangement of several objects from around the house and look at the world from a different angle to inspire art.

50. Collage, draw, paint, and/or write on top of copies of old photos.

51. Art can be great fun when two people work at it together, so find a partner (or two, or three) and collaborate, encourage, and create.

52. Go on the Internet and search for people to share with, words to be inspired by, and images to get your mind spinning.

Remember, cross-training is a valuable tool, and loads of fun, too!

Soon you will receive pleasant news

Be mischievous and you will not be lonesome

Grand adventures await those who are willing to turn the corner

A closed mouth gathers no feet

A warm smile is testimony of a generous nature

Soon you will be sitting on top of the world

Be prepared to accept a wondrous opportunity in the days ahead!

The time is right to make new friends

Get ready! Good fortune comes in bunches

Fast-Piece Appliqué Basics

In this section, you'll learn the basics of Fast-Piece Appliqué construction. By following the step-by-step process you'll quickly learn how this method lets you make easy work of sewing curves, circles, and many other shapes that you thought were too difficult to piece together.

Once learned, Fast-Pieced Appliqué may be used on its own or in combination with a multitude of other construction methods. The projects in this book were created to show how this method can be used to stitch the most simple to the most complex designs and, of course, how to mix-it-all-up. Enjoy creating the quilts in this book and incorporating Fast-Pieced Appliqué into your next quilt project!

Enlarging and Using Patterns

All of the projects in this book need to be enlarged to create the finished size shown. There are many ways to enlarge a pattern, but if you find yourself without technology, such as a computer, opaque projector, or copier, there is always the old reliable grid method. You can also use this method for any design you create on your own.

GRID METHOD

To use this quick and simple way to enlarge a pattern, follow these steps. You'll need a pencil, a piece of tracing paper slightly larger than the size of the pattern in this book, and a piece of tracing paper the finished size of the project.

1. Using a pencil, trace the pattern from the book directly onto the smaller piece of tracing paper. Cut out the pattern on the outer line.

2. Fold the pattern in half vertically, and then fold in half vertically again.

3. Turn the pattern 90°, and then fold it in half horizontally. Fold it in half horizontally again. Unfold the pattern. The fold lines have created a grid.

4. Repeat the folding process with the larger piece of tracing paper. When both patterns are unfolded, you'll have the same number of grid lines on both papers.

5. Now look at one section of the grid with the pattern, and draw what you see in the corresponding section of the larger grid. I start at the upper-left section of the pattern, and after the first section is enlarged I go on to the next section, working left to right and top to bottom until everything is enlarged. If there are changes or corrections, I make them with pencil at this point.

Original drawing or copy of the pattern from the book, folded to create grid

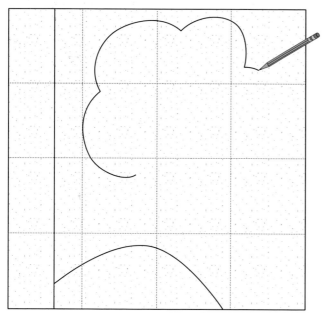

Tracing paper cut to the finished size of the quilt, folded to create grid, and ready for copying

6. After all the lines are successfully drawn onto the larger grid, go over each with a fine-point permanent marker. Transfer the number of each pattern piece or shape onto the tracing-paper pattern. Add hash marks (short lines drawn across the pattern lines) along the lines between shapes.

Preparing the Freezer-Paper Pattern

After the tracing-paper pattern is complete, you'll need to make a freezer-paper pattern. The freezer-paper drawing will be the pattern. It will be used to cut out the fabrics and as a sewing guide when joining the pieces. The tracing-paper pattern will remain intact and be used as a placement guide.

1. Cut a piece of freezer paper the same size as your tracing-paper pattern. (See the tip box below for instructions on how to join freezer-paper sheets as needed to make larger patterns.)

2. Place the freezer paper over the tracing-paper pattern, shiny side down.

3. Using the permanent marker again, trace the lines, numbers, and hash marks onto the freezer paper.

PREPARING LARGER FREEZER-PAPER SHEETS

When working with a larger design, prepare the freezer paper as follows to achieve the required size. By applying adhesive between the two layers, you'll be able to iron the freezer paper as needed during the sewing process without worrying about burning tape or glue.

1. Lay two sheets of freezer paper flat on a table, overlapping the edges about 1".

2. Using either permanent double-stick tape or a permanent glue stick, apply adhesive to the area between the overlapping layers. Press the pieces together with your fingers.

Two layers of freezer paper aligned and ready for applying adhesive

Selecting and Marking the Fabrics

After the tracing-paper and freezer-paper patterns are completed, the fun begins. Now you need to select a fabric for each numbered pattern piece of the quilt top. As each fabric is selected, it's best to mark the fabric with its corresponding pattern-piece number. I use numbered pieces of masking tape.

1. Lay a strip of masking tape on your cutting mat.

2. With a marker, write a number for each of the pattern shapes. For example, if there are 42 shapes, mark each number from 1 to 42 on the tape.

3. With your rotary cutter, cut apart the tape between the numbers.

4. Select a fabric for piece 1 on your pattern, and then place the tape marker for piece 1 on the fabric. Repeat this process with the remaining shapes and numbers.

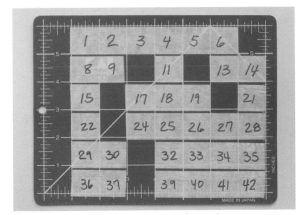

Masking-tape numbers provide a fast and easy way to keep track of your fabric selections. When all the numbers are gone, all the fabrics have been selected.

Preparing the Pattern for Sewing

Once you've selected the fabrics, you can prepare each of the various pattern pieces for sewing.

1. Cut apart the freezer-paper pattern by cutting directly on the lines.

2. Match the pattern number to the fabric chosen for that pattern piece.

3. Iron the freezer-paper pattern piece (shiny side down) onto the right side of the corresponding numbered fabric. Make sure to remove the masking-tape number before ironing the shape in place!

4. Cut out each fabric piece, leaving ½" extra around the entire template for seam allowance.

Constructing the Quilt Top

Set your sewing machine for straight stitching. Use a neutral thread (beige, gray, and black are good choices) on the top and in the bobbin. The thread should be visible but not highly contrasting.

1. Select two fabric pieces adjacent to each other in the design. The instructions for each project will give you the assembly order. Place them together side by side on your ironing board.

2. Butt the edges of the templates together using the hash marks for alignment. To do this, you'll need to lift up one template edge and slide the seam allowance of the other fabric piece under it (see "Light and Dark Fabric" below).

3. Once the pieces are lined up, slightly separate them, leaving only the width of a sewing-machine needle between the edges of the two templates. Iron the freezer-paper pattern templates back into place.

4. Following the pattern pieces, sew in the space between the two shapes.

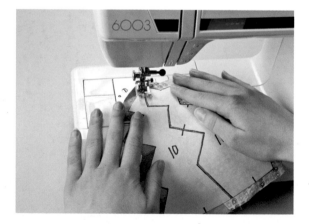

LIGHT AND DARK FABRIC

When joining a very light fabric to a dark one, lift the freezer-paper template from the light fabric and slide the seam allowance of the dark fabric on top of it. This will eliminate any shadows that could possibly be seen through the light fabric.

5. After sewing the two pieces together, lift up the edge of the freezer-paper template from the fabric that is on the bottom, exposing the stitching line and the raw edge of the fabric that is on top. Lift only enough for trimming the excess fabric.

6. Trim the excess top fabric as close to the stitching line as possible using duckbill appliqué scissors. Trim only along the stitching line on top; don't trim the bottom fabric.

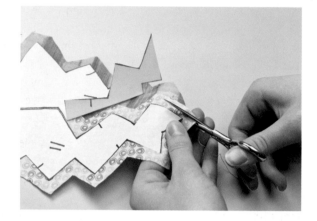

7. Once the fabric is trimmed, iron the freezer paper back into place.

8. Continue sewing pattern pieces together in this manner to create sections. Then sew the sections together in the same manner to complete the top. Leave the templates in place.

FAST SEWING WITH CHAIN STITCHING

Chain stitching is a great method to use when sewing larger quilt tops together. It makes the process faster, while saving time and thread. With the pattern pieces laid out on the tracing-paper guide, choose pairs of pieces from various locations. (The pairs are identified in the instructions for each project.) Once you've chosen several pairs, place each pair on your ironing board and prepare it for stitching.

Feed the first prepared pair under the presser foot. Once the first pair is almost completely stitched, slide the next pair in place and continue stitching. Keep in mind that smaller pieces will build into larger sections, so always pay attention to the tracing-paper guide to ensure the sewing is as direct as possible.

Couching, Quilting, and Finishing Basics

With the quilt top finished, it's time to move on to making a quilt sandwich and stitching everything together. Many of the quilts in this book are designed and sized to hang on the wall and to be embellished with beads and other objects that add weight to the quilt. Even otherwise-sized quilts call for the use of thin batting. Thin batting tends to be lightweight and easily stitched. There are many battings of this type on the market and manufacturers continue to improve on the quality of these products.

When it comes to the backing fabric, I generally select a good cotton fabric that's easy to stitch through whether by machine or by hand. Good cotton fabric doesn't have to mean boring; I love to make the backing from a wild print that coordinates with my quilt top. This is also a great place to use scraps from the top! The backing can add fun and excitement, with the added benefit of concealing a multitude of possibly not-so-perfect quilting stitches. Have fun with this fabric! Don't be afraid to try the wild and crazy. Even strong directional prints can be the perfect choice.

Preparing the Quilt Sandwich

1. Lay the ironed backing fabric right side down on a flat surface and use masking tape to secure it in place.

2. Carefully remove the freezer-paper templates and press the quilt top.

3. Center the batting on the backing fabric. Center the top, right side up, on the batting. Tape the batting and top in place.

4. Secure the layers using safety pins every few inches.

SETTING UP YOUR MACHINE FOR COUCHING

You'll be couching yarn along all the raw edges of your quilt design to cover up the stitching lines and to delineate the shapes.

1. Select yarns for couching that coordinate with your quilt-top fabrics.

2. Thread the sewing-machine needle with a decorative thread, such as metallic or rayon, that will work with the yarns you're planning to use. Wind the bobbin with a thread that will look nice on the back of the quilt and is compatible with the top thread.

Use safety pins to baste the quilt sandwich.

3. Feed the selected yarn through the foot opening. If you're using an open-toe foot, hold the yarn in place below the opening.

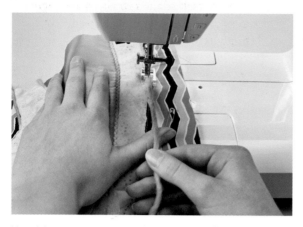

Use either an open-toe stitching or braiding/cording/couching foot for machine couching.

4. Set your machine for a zigzag stitch. Set the stitch length to zero and the width to 3 or 3.5 mm.

5. Start sewing at the edge and take about four stitches in place to lock the stitch.

6. Reset the stitch length to 3.5 mm. Continue stitching, couching the yarn over the seam line so that it covers the raw edges of the fabric and the stitching line. Remove any safety pins that are in the line of stitching as you go.

7. At the end of the line, reset the stitch length back to zero and take several stitches in place to lock the thread.

8. Continue couching over all the raw edges, removing the safety pins as you stitch.

9. When all the couching is done, remove the remaining pins and press the quilt from the back.

Quilting

The couching acts as quilting to hold the layers together, but now is the time to add machine or hand quilting, if desired.

The quilting stitch, whether by machine or by hand, is an extra element of design that can be incorporated into the quilt. Earlier, I mentioned falling for those little stitches made so carefully on the traditional Amish quilts. The Amish were not alone in using quilting as an important element in their quilt designs. Traditional Hawaiian quilters used line to great advantage. In my mind they are the "echo" quilters. I know this is an overstatement, since historically echo quilting has been around for a very long time.

Whenever possible, the first couched line should start at one quilt edge and run through the center of the quilt from top to bottom or side to side. Then work from that center point toward the outside edges. If there's no stitching line running completely across the quilt, start at a point near the center and work out toward the edges of the quilt.

Practice couching on a sample sandwich first to check the stitch quality. Stitch at least 3" on your sample and check the stitching on both the top and the back.

- If the bobbin thread is showing through on the top, loosen the tension (lower the number).

- If the top thread is showing through on the back, increase the tension (raise the number).

- Let the sewing machine stitch at its own pace; don't force the fabric through.

- If the yarn and stitching begin to bunch or tighten, increase the length (not the width) of the zigzag stitch.

- Running the yarn through a ½" piece of plastic straw attached to the upper-right front of your machine will help keep the yarn out of the way as you couch.

- To create a sharp point or corner, take one extra stitch in place just before you turn the corner.

- If you slightly miss covering over the stitching line, use a fabric marker in a color similar to the yarn to cover the line.

The point I want to make is that a simple line is a powerful thing. As I mentioned in "Starting at the Beginning—The Basic Line" on page 24, there are many factors that come into play when you consider how to add line to your design. It's a great way to artify your quilt.

In my previous books, I have suggested looking for quilting inspiration in nature, which will always be an invaluable source. Whether thinking about the veining in leaves, grasses blowing in the wind, the bumps of bark on a tree, or fluffy cloud formations, the quilting line is a way to bring the textural wonder to a quilt whether by its presence or absence (see "It All Starts to Take Shape" on page 34).

Once you've decide on a quilting design (or your quilt tells you what it wants), you're ready to transfer the design to the quilt. I recommend using a chalk liner tool (this has a wheel that lays down the chalk) to block out areas where you want a specific pattern. This tool allows you to easily mark the quilt and then stand back to preview the stitching areas before making the final decision on where to place your quilting. The chalk remains visible while you work on the quilting, but is easily dusted off when you're done.

When creating a new machine-quilting motif, I recommend that you practice drawing it out on paper. This creates a memory connection between your hand and your mind, so that when you begin to machine quilt your hand knows the motion required to create your quilting pattern. It also helps to hang the practice drawing above your sewing machine as a guide.

Binding

After your quilt is couched and quilted, it's time to add the binding. You have many binding options, two of which I've included here. One is a traditional, double-fold binding, and the other is my favorite because it pulls everything to the back and leaves a very nice, clean edge.

STANDARD BINDING

To finish off the quilt traditionally, use a double-fold binding. It nicely frames the quilt.

1. Square up the quilt.

2. Cut 2"-wide straight-grain strips (selvage to selvage) from the binding fabric. You will need enough strips to go around the quilt plus approximately 10" additional for joining strips and mitering corners.

3. With right sides together, join the strips end to end to make one long strip.

4. Trim one end of the strip at a 45° angle and press the raw angled end under ¼". This will be the beginning of the binding strip.

5. Fold the binding strip in half lengthwise, wrong sides together, and press. Your strip should now be 1" wide.

6. Starting in the middle of one side of the layered quilt, lay the binding strip along the edge of the quilt top, raw edges aligned. Using a ¼" seam allowance, stitch the binding to the quilt, beginning several inches from the angled end. Stop sewing ¼" from the first corner; backstitch. Cut the threads and remove the quilt from the machine.

7. Rotate the quilt so you are ready to sew the next edge. Fold the binding up at a 90° angle so the fold makes a 45° angle. Fold the binding back down onto itself so the raw edges are aligned. Begin stitching at the edge, backstitch, and then continue until you're ¼" from the next corner; backstitch. Repeat the folding and stitching process at each corner.

Fold the binding strip up so the fold makes a 45° angle.

Fold the binding back down onto itself, aligning the binding and quilt raw edges.

8. When you are close to the beginning of the binding, trim the end of the strip so it overlaps the beginning by approximately 1". Continue sewing the binding in place.

9. Add any desired dimensional stitching and beading.

10. Fold the binding to the back of the quilt and hand stitch the folded edge in place, covering the machine stitching.

FACED BINDING

Use this binding option when you don't want to see binding fabric on the front of the finished quilt.

1. Square up the quilt.

2. Cut 4½"-wide straight-grain strips (selvage to selvage) from the binding fabric. You'll need four strips, one for each edge of the quilt. Add 2" to the length of each side of the quilt and cut the binding strips to that length. (For sides longer than 40", join strips end to end with right sides together to get the length needed.)

3. Fold each binding strip in half lengthwise with wrong sides together and press. The strips should now be 2¼" wide.

4. With right sides together and raw edges aligned, pin a binding strip along the top edge of the quilt, leaving about 1" extending beyond each corner.

5. With a neutral thread in the sewing machine, begin sewing ¼" from the corner, backstitch, and then stitch using a ¼" seam allowance. Sew until you are ¼" from the next corner and backstitch.

6. Repeat step 5 along the bottom edge of the quilt. Press the binding and seam allowance outward so they lie flat.

Sew the binding to the top and bottom edges; press.

7. In the same manner, sew binding strips to the remaining two sides of the quilt; press.

Stitch binding strips to the side edges; press.

8. After all sides are sewn and pressed, snip a small triangle of batting, backing, and quilt top off each corner to reduce bulk.

9. To turn the binding to the back, start at the top edge and fold the binding fabric toward the back of the quilt. Iron, trim the excess binding along the sides, and pin in place.

10. Stitch this length of the binding in place by hand. Repeat along the bottom edge. Press the binding from the back of the quilt.

11. Trim excess fabric from the side binding strips so that ¼" extends beyond the sides. Fold the binding to the back of the quilt on each side. Iron, and pin in place.

12. Turn under the ¼" of fabric at each corner and tuck it in so that the edge is even with the previously sewn edge; pin in place.

Turn back the corner and tuck in the excess fabric.

13. Repeat to turn under the binding fabric at all corners and hand sew the remaining binding to the backing.

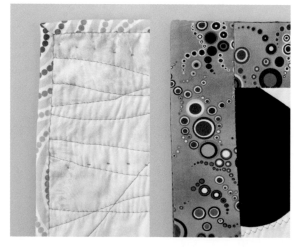

Standard binding is on the left and faced binding is on the right.

Resources

Fabric

Andover Fabrics Inc.

1384 Broadway, Ste. 1500
New York, NY 10018
800-223-5678

Anthology Fabrics

14745 Carmenita Rd.
Norwalk, CA 90650
800-450-2030
www.anthologyfabrics.com

Robert Kaufman Fabrics

Box 59266, Greenmead Station
Los Angeles, CA 90059-0266
800-877-2066
www.robertkaufman.com

Quilting Treasures

1381 Cranston St.
Cranston, RI 02920
800-876-2756
www.quiltingtreasures.com

Spoonflower Inc.

2810 Meridian Parkway, Ste. 130
Durham, NC 27713
919-886-7885
www.spoonflower.com

Thread

Aurifil USA

184 Shuman Boulevard, Ste. 200
Naperville, IL 60563
312-212-3485
www.aurifilusa.com

Kreinik Manufacturing Co. Inc.

1708 Gihon Road
Parkersburg, WV 26102
800-624-1928
www.kreinik.com

Superior Threads

87 East 2580 South
St. George, UT 84790
800-499-1777
www.superiorthreads.com

General Sewing Notions

Therm-O-Web Adhesives

770 Glenn Avenue
Wheeling, IL 60090
800-323-0799
www.thermowebonline.com

General Art Supplies

Art Supply Warehouse

6672 Westminster Blvd.
Westminster, CA 92683
800-854-6467
www.artsupplywarehouse.com

Blick Art Materials

P.O. Box 1267
Galesburg, IL 61402-1267
800-828-4548
www.dickblick.com

Jacquard Products

Ruper, Gibbon and Spider Inc.
PO Box 425
Healdsburg, CA 95448
800-442-0455
www.jacquardproducts.com

By Annie

Annie Unrein
P.O. Box 1003
St. George, UT 84771-1003
435-674-9816
www.byannie.com

About the Author

After 20 years in the corporate world, Rose Hughes jumped into her quilt art life in 2003 and has never looked back. Her love of photography continues to inspire her stitching journey, and in this book Rose feels like she is coming full circle to some of the favorite "fabricy" things that made her pick up a needle. This time she mixes up the older loves with her Fast-Piece Appliqué construction method, introduced in her first book, *Dream Landscapes: Artful Quilts with Fast-Piece Appliqué* (Martingale, 2008). Never one to leave out the shine, Rose also mixes in ideas found in her second book, *Exploring Embellishments* (Martingale, 2010).

Rose loves to share her quilting passions and travels the world providing entertaining and educational lectures. Her teaching topics include Fast-Piece Appliqué (of course), but her lineup of workshops also covers design, fabric painting, color, and all forms of embellishment!

As Rose continues to pursue her own art, you may find her quilts in juried exhibitions throughout the world, but you may also click on the television or computer and find her sharing her work and methods. She enjoys membership in numerous quilt- and art-related organizations and finds joy in sharing her love of the art of quilting through her blog, ravenspeakquilts.blogspot.com; her website, www.rosehughes.com; and her Facebook page.

photo credit Carlo Parducho